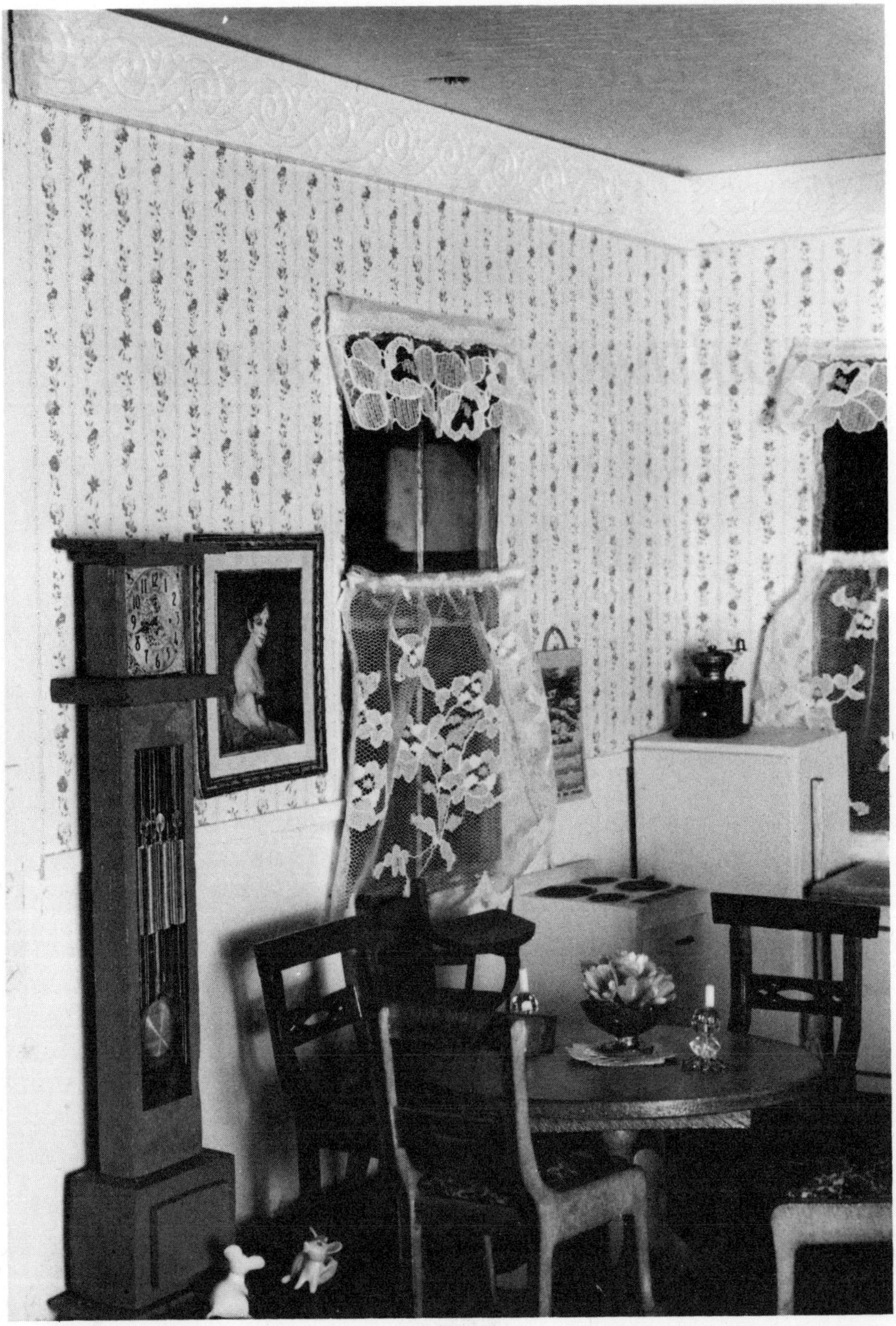

Dollhouse Accessories
How To Design and Make Them

by
Margaret B. Duda
Photography by Jon Sheckler

SOUTH BRUNSWICK AND NEW YORK: A. S. BARNES AND COMPANY
LONDON: THOMAS YOSELOFF LTD

© 1975 by Margaret B. Duda

A. S. Barnes and Co., Inc.
Cranbury, New Jersey 08512

Thomas Yoseloff Ltd
108 New Bond Street
London W1Y OQX, England

Library of Congress Cataloging in Publication Data

Duda, Margaret B
   Dollhouse accessories.

   Bibliography: p.
   1. Doll-houses. 2. Doll furniture. I. Title.
TT175.3.D82   745.59'23   74-9281
ISBN 0-498-01557-2

First printing March, 1975
Second printing March, 1976

Dedicated to:

John, David, Paul, and Laura,
without whose interest this book may never
have been written.

PRINTED IN THE UNITED STATES OF AMERICA

Contents

  Acknowledgments
  Introduction   11
  Materials   17
1 Play Food from Play Dough   21
2 Things for the Table   33
3 Household Necessities   41
4 Windows, Wall, and Floor Coverings   59
5 Accessories for the Cultured Family   72
6 Homes for Household Pets   85
7 Outdoor Accessories   95
8 Furniture   109
  Summary   127
  Bibliography   129

Acknowledgments

I wish to extend my gratitude to Jon Sheckler for his tireless patience in photographing my miniatures; to Julia Reed for her generosity in sharing her time, creative ideas, and infectious enthusiasm; and most of all, to my husband, Larry, and my four children, all of whom agreed to share my time with this book.

Introduction

There was a time when only the very rich could afford an elaborate dollhouse, and it seemed to follow that the richer the owner, the more complete the dollhouse. The earliest dollhouse on record is one ordered by Duke Albrecht V of Bavaria for his small daughter in 1558. It was four-stories high and had seventeen doors, sixty-three windows, and everything from a stable in the bottom level to a ballroom at the top. Already there were such things as embroidered tapestries and rich carpets and gold and silver dishes on the buffet. There were spinning wheels and silver lutes and andirons by the fireplace. More and more craftsmen were called upon to add miniature accessories and the dollhouse turned into such a wonder that the Duke finally had it put into his art collection instead!

After this earliest creation came multitudes of dollhouses, most of them commissioned by the wealthy. Many of these dollhouses became art objects because they were representative of their period in history. My own interest in miniatures had no such elaborate beginnings. Like many other children in middle-class families during the 1950s, I had a metal dollhouse with plastic furniture that lent itself to story creations, but not to interior decoration.

Then one day, one of our neighbors, a lovely lady in her midseventies, asked me if I would like to have an old wooden dollhouse that had belonged to her daughter, who no longer wanted it. The dollhouse had been stored for years and was badly in need of a coat of paint, but it was unlike any dollhouse I had ever seen before. It was almost three-

The basic dollhouse was a gift.

feet tall with high ceilings and real glass windows. It had three stories, a front porch, and you opened two doors at the back to look inside. There was a large room on the bottom floor, two on the second, and another on the third. There were some odds and ends of wooden furniture thrown into corners, but the greatest surprise was the fact that it had electric lights wired into the ceilings!

My mother looked at the house doubtfully, but it had already cast its spell on me and I couldn't wait to get home and start redecorating. There were curtains to be made and rugs to be found for the bare, wooden floors. The tables needed cloths and the beds needed spreads. And that was just the beginning! My first efforts were crude ones, to say the least, but I continued to work on the dollhouse into my teens when I finally found boys more interesting and put it into storage.

I never could forget the dollhouse, however, and when I got married, I took it with me. When I was expecting our first child, I thought of redoing the house for a daughter, but twins, John and Dave, entered our lives and I forgot it as I prepared formulas and wondered at the beauty of healthy sons. When the twins were a year-and-a-half old, loveable Paul joined the family and once more, thoughts of the dollhouse were pushed aside. Finally, when Paul was almost two, Laura Margaret made her way into our household and miniature accessory possibilities slowly emerged from my subconscious.

With four preschoolers, the dollhouse was never resurrected until Laura was four years old. Then I found that during one of our many moves, a window had been broken and a porch pillar had gotten lost. My father-in-law, a cabinetmaker, replaced the pillar and built a new stairway to the second floor. My husband then made a platform base on small legs for the house so that Laura could have a "yard" and could reach the first floor more easily. That's when my imagination took over. Miniature-scaled wallpaper was found and the rooms were carpeted and the windows draped. I refinished the wooden pieces of furniture that needed it and bought new pieces to replace many of my childhood plastic items that I found had warped with the years.

Finally, all was in readiness, but something was still missing. I had seen pictures and read books about famous dollhouses and knew that ours lacked the fascination of the more elaborate ones. Then I knew. The things that made dollhouses fascinating for both those playing or those just looking are the miniature accessories. I suddenly realized that the more crowded a dollhouse was with appropriately scaled miniatures, the more interesting it was.

At first we invested in things from private dealers who advertised in craft magazines. In buying these artistic creations, we soon discovered that the size of the item had no relation to its price. In fact, the smaller the item, the more expensive it seemed to be, and many of the miniature accessories cost more than their full-sized counterparts!

Since we could not afford to buy all of the things we wanted, I had to find another way to get them. I asked my daughter, who by this time had turned six, "Why not try to make some things?" With that question, and her excited reply, began hours of creative fun that I could share with her. The more things we made, the more ideas we got, and the more excited we became. Soon we were looking at everything in terms of miniature possibilities. The beauty of making these accessories is that your child can help. My daughter soon learned to develop accessories from ideas of her own and she will probably treasure those created items more than the ones we bought, because she made them herself.

Dollhouses are not the only places for these miniatures. As one can see by the many advertisements in magazines, miniatures are one of the fastest-growing hobbies in the United States. One no longer needs to have an elaborate dollhouse, and many people start with shadow boxes (9½ inches high by 14 inches wide by 5 inches deep) and furnish a single room. These rooms are usually representative of a certain period in history, since miniature reproductions are available in many styles of furniture. Once you have the furniture, you can start decorating with accessories. Many accessories will fit any period. Even in the earliest days of our country, there were pies and paintings and serving dishes. Many collectors also enjoy furnishing small rooms to resemble shops. General stores are popular, as well as antique shops, bakeries, and one-room school houses. The possibilities are as varied as one's imagination, but one thing is certain. Whatever you choose, you will need accessories.

Although an interest in miniatures is no longer limited to the very rich, there are still some accessories that most private collectors could not duplicate. There is the chandelier in Colleen Moore's Fairy Castle at Chicago's Museum of Science and Industry that was made of her diamonds, emeralds, and pearls. There is also a dollhouse from the Civil War period at the Historical Society of Delaware in Wilmington, which has an art gallery filled with miniature oil and water color paintings by well-known Philadelphia artists of the period. But things like these are not to be played with or even touched. Most little girls and even adults would rather have accessories that can be felt and moved to recreate lifelike situations. There are easy, inexpensive ways to make these things as you will see on the following pages. Wherever possible, the scale used is approximately 1 inch to 1 foot. I have tried to cut down the cost of volume packages by using many of the same materials in different items. But I warn you, creativity is contagious. From our ideas, you will probably develop many of your own. All you have to do is think small and see possibilities in miniature.

My daughter, Laura, and the dollhouse

Materials

THINGS FOUND IN A HARDWARE STORE

wooden dowels, metal nuts, flexible wire, ceiling adapters, silicone glue, sandpaper, epoxy cement, brass finials, plastic suction cups, masking tape, brass chain, eye screws, staple nails, tacks, hammer, contact paper, rubber faucet washers, tin snips, brass nails

THINGS FOUND IN A FABRIC STORE

material, buttons, heavy weight and regular thread, netting, horsehair lining, felt ribbon, hemming tape

THINGS FOUND IN A GROCERY STORE

colored sugar toppings, nonpareils, plastic salt shakers, plastic pumpkin (in the bakery section)

THINGS FOUND IN A HOBBY SHOP

X-acto knife set (a handle with small exchangable blades for making various kinds of cuts), balsa wood, clay, flexible wire, Christmas trees, white glue, mosaic tiles, plastic suction cups, matting board, felt-tip pens, beads, bead caps, shells, artificial flowers, wooden dowels, feathers

THINGS FOUND IN DRUG STORES

pushpins, masking tape, matting board, white glue, mounting squares, two-sided tape, felt-tip pens

SPECIALTY ITEMS

wallpaper paste—paint store
miniature baskets—toy shop
oasis—florist's shop
aluminum caning and pine moulding—lumber dealer
carpet samples—carpet shop or department store that carries carpeting
buttons in graduated sizes—dry cleaners or fabric store
miniature-scaled wallpaper—private dealers who advertise in craft magazines

Dollhouse Accessories
How To Design
and Make Them

1
Play Food from Play Dough

One of the first things that strikes a dollhouse owner is the amount of food it takes to sustain a miniature family. Not only do they eat everyday fare, but they must also be supplied for holidays and special outings. There are birthday parties for the children and picnics during the summer and a feast at Thanksgiving. The mother is kept busy in the kitchen, as many a dollhouse family eats better than their adult counterparts. How then to settle all these needs?

Prepackaged foods are available in expensive toy shops but a large supply of these might compare with your weekly grocery bill. The simplest and cheapest way to stock a kitchen is to make your own food.

There are two simple bases for play food. You can make your own mixture or you can use Play-Doh. There are advantages and disadvantages to each one. If you use Play-Doh, you won't have to prepare anything before you start to shape your food. It also stays rubbery a long time, allowing for changes in the shapes. There is one big disadvantage to Play-Doh, however, and that is the fact that it shrinks as it dries out. You therefore have to allow for this shrinkage.

The homemade mixture is the traditional bread dough used in many craft projects. Although there is some work to prepare your dough, you may store it in the refrigerator in a plastic bag for future projects.

For your homemade bread dough, you will need:

3 slices of white bread
3 tablespoons of white glue
3 drops of lemon juice

Remove the crusts from the bread, crumble onto a flat plate, and add the glue and lemon juice. Knead this mixture until the texture resembles regular dough and no longer sticks to your fingers. Now you are ready to shape your food.

Whether you use Play-Doh or bread dough, you will probably want to paint your food to make them look realistic. Acrylic paints or watercolors will give you more variety in your tones and should be used for items such as baked goods and meats, while model enamel will give the necessary brightness to your fruits and vegetables. Whichever one you use, I would recommend varnishing for a lasting finish, and this will also cut down on the shrinkage.

Try the foods on the following pages, then go on to make some of your own household favorites.

BREAKFAST PLATE

The right way to begin a day is with a hearty breakfast and this one is hard to beat. To begin the meal, there is half a grapefruit made by flattening one side of a small ball of dough and by painting the appropriate colors. The sections are black lines painted over the flesh-toned pulp. For the eggs, flatten a piece of dough into a figure eight. Then press two flat yolks into the middle of each egg and paint them white and yellow. The bacon is made from the strips cut off the toast to make it square, then pushed together to curl slightly, and painted brownish red. The toast is painted a light brown, then given a darker crust as a finishing touch. All of these items were varnished.

LOAVES OF BREAD

Despite Women's Lib, most miniature dollhouse mothers are still great bakers and bread is usually one of their specialties. For our regular loaf, we shaped a piece of dough into a rectangular shape about a half-inch thick. Stand the loaf on one of the long ends and pull the four

Breakfast Plate

Loaves of Bread

edges of the top down to form an upper crust. This also makes a slight bulge in the top of the loaf. Paint the top brown with watercolors and the sides a lighter shade by mixing dark orange and yellow. Varnish to prevent much shrinkage. For the Italian loaf of bread, shape your dough into a long thin loaf and make diagonal creases with the edge of a small paintbrush handle. Paint light brown and varnish.

BAKED HAM AND ROAST TURKEY

Most holidays and Sunday meals require special meats and here we find two favorites. For the roast turkey, start with a round ball of dough. Flatten one side, making the base broader, and lengthen slightly. Pull the breast of the turkey into shape on the top. For the legs and wings, use the handle of a small paintbrush and make curved indentations. For the legs, start in the middle of the side and go backwards, pressing toward the top, then back to the tail of the turkey. For the wings, make smaller indentations, pressing toward the neck. Paint a dark orange brown,

Baked Ham and Roast Turkey

Pies

making the top of the breast and the legs darker as they would be after baking.

For the ham, form the dough into the proper shape and paint dark brown for the outside and dark pink for the center. An interesting variation of this piece is to make it on a plate with a slice already cut.

Varnish both pieces.

PIES

No feast or bakery shop is complete without a pie and you can have a variety with my simple recipe. For your pan, use a soda-bottle cap. Paint with silver enamel on the outside. Simply fill the bottle cap with dough, making a mound in the middle. Overlap the edges of the bottle cap to allow for shrinkage if you're using the Play-Doh. Use less with the bread dough. Then, with a toothpick, make indentations around the edge of the pie, as you would with a fork on a real one, and make several small "slits" in the middle. Next, paint the pie with a mixture of yellow and orange watercolors. Let dry and varnish.

Corn on the Cob and Baked Potatoes

To make the fruit pie, follow the same procedure for filling the bottle cap "pan." Then cut a slice out of the pie and proceed as before with the toothpick. The difference comes in the painting. Paint the inside of the pie, which is now showing, either purple for blueberry or red for cherry, and paint the slits in the upper crust as well. Then paint the crust as before and varnish.

CORN ON THE COB AND BAKED POTATOES

Every feast needs vegetables to go with the meat and, whether it's a picnic or a family dinner, these two items are sure to please the palates of a miniature family. For the baked potatoes, simply roll the dough into the shape of potatoes, making them different sizes, and paint medium brown. The potatoes should be varnished, then glued together inside a bowl.

The corn on the cob takes a little more work. After you have formed the cob shapes, make indentations with the point of a toothpick, giving

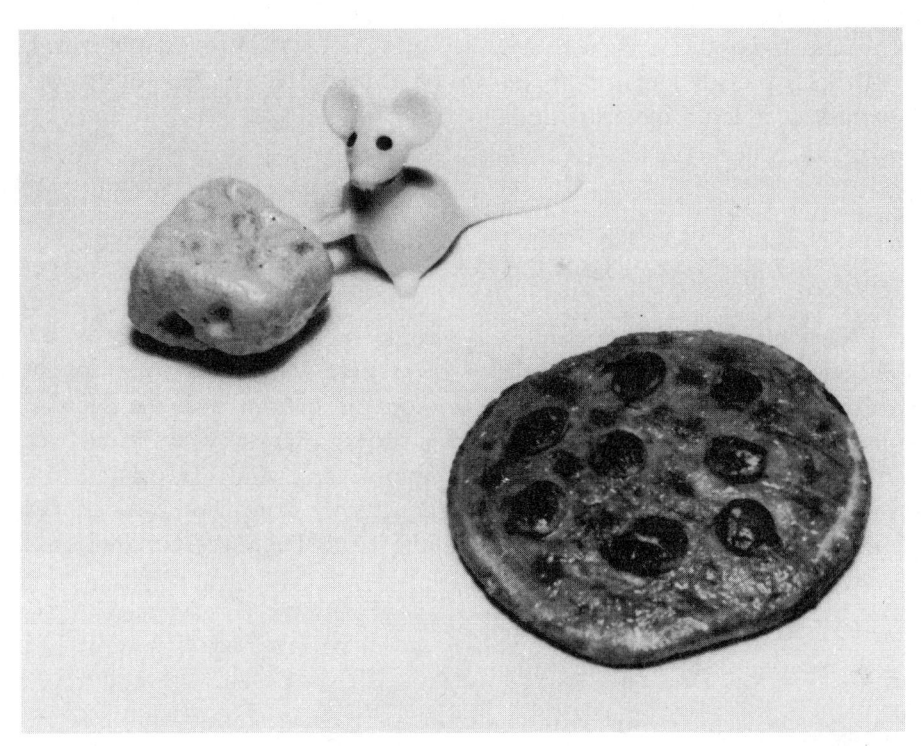

Pizza and Swiss Cheese

the effect of lumpy corn. Then make holders from slivers of balsa wood and put one into each end of the corn. Paint bright yellow, varnish, and glue together into the shape of a stack on a plate. If you try hard, you can almost see the steam rising as you set the vegetables on the table.

PIZZA AND SWISS CHEESE

Here is a must for evening snacks or a quick, pick-me-up dinner when the dollhouse mother has had a hard day. Our pizza is one with pepperoni, but you can also make them plain, with green peppers, or with ground meat. All start with a basic ball of dough flattened into the shape of a round pizza. The pepperoni was made by flattening tiny balls of dough and sticking them onto the top. The full effect comes with the painting, and watercolor is best for this one. The shell should be skin colored, the pizza dark red, and the pepperoni dark brown. Varnishing brings out the contrasts and also makes sure the pepperoni stays in place. For variety, you might try making one with a slice missing.

The swiss cheese, which is so tempting to our little mouse friend, had holes pressed into it with the tip of a toothpick. Painted yellow and varnished, it looks most inviting.

BIRTHDAY CAKE

One quickly finds that birthdays come more than once a year for dollhouse members. For a birthday cake, start with a circle of dough, roll into a cake shape by flattening the top and bottom with the flat side of a knife, and roll the sides on a flat surface. Spread white glue over the top and sides of the cake and roll into sugar crystals (a colored topping), which may be purchased in the grocery store. For candles, cut pieces of balsa wood and insert into the cake. Paint the tips red, and you're ready for a party.

Birthday Cake

Jelly Roll and Brownies

JELLY ROLL AND BROWNIES

Most dollhouse mothers are very considerate of their family's tastes and jelly roll is a favorite with our hard-working father, while the children choose brownies every time. For the jelly roll, put one flat circle of dough on top of another and roll into the form of a jelly roll. Paint the top and ends brown, allowing the white "cream" to show on the sides. Varnish, making sure to get the white in between the layers.

For the brownies, form a square of dough and make sectional indentations with the side of a toothpick. If you're very ambitious, cut off several squares. Paint dark brown and varnish.

FRUIT BOWL

A fruit bowl used as a centerpiece makes every table inviting. My bowl was a special find at an antique sale, but you can use plastic suction cups with flat bottoms found in any hobby store. The fruit was simply

Fruit Bowl

shaped, then painted the appropriate colors. A stem made of a sliver of balsa wood was inserted into the apples. The grapes are the only real problem. I recommend rolling each grape individually, then forming two, flat-sided "bunches" by gluing each side of the bunch onto pieces of cardboard, and painting. When each side has dried, cut the cardboard around the grapes, turn over and glue the sides of the bunches together. Bright enamels make the individual fruits stand out.

CAKES AND COOKIES

Cakes and cookies are necessities for bakeries and dollhouse children returning from school. Our cookies are both plain and frosted for variety on the plate. To make them, roll your dough into little balls and press flat with a knife. Then paint a light brown, followed by another color if you want them "frosted." Varnish and then glue the arrangement to a plate, since these will easily get lost.

For an iced cake that shows its flavor, make the cake shape as you did for the birthday cake. Then cut a slice from the middle. Paint the

Cakes and Cookies

Watermelon and Candied Apples

outside one of the many icing colors and the inside a light yellow, white, or brown. For a white or yellow layer cake, paint a black line to show the layers; for a chocolate cake, make it white. Varnish.

WATERMELON AND CANDIED APPLES

No picnic is complete without a watermelon and ours is fat and juicy. Start with a shape the size of a whole watermelon and flatten one side. Paint the outside dark green with spots of white and the inside a dark red with dots of black for the seeds. Varnish.

Our candied apples are special treats for very good children. Small balls of dough form the apples, which are slightly flattened at each end with a toothpick. Slivers of balsa wood make the sticks and these may be held when painting the apples bright red. For drying, place the stick into a ball of dough; the apples may be varnished in this manner, also.

2
Things for the Table

Miniature dining tables come in many shapes and sizes. There are round ones and square ones and oblong ones. There are Duncan Phyfe tables and Queen Anne tables and Shaker-style tables. There are dining-room tables and kitchen tables and picnic tables. But all of them have one thing in common. Miniature families must have one to eat on and, whichever style you choose for your dollhouse or miniature scene, you will soon find yourself in need of some accessories.

An eating table has two basic uses. It is utilitarian when it comes to meals and snacks, but it is also a decorative piece of furniture when not in use and needs some ornamentation. We have found means to solve both of these problems.

Now that you have your food, you will need dishes and goblets and necessities like salt and pepper shakers. For regular meals, there are place mats, while formal dinners rate crystal candlesticks and flower bowls. Whether it's a meal inside or a picnic outside, these accessories will help to make the meal more inviting and the centerpiece will do wonders for a table at rest.

DISHES

Dishes are a necessity on dollhouse tables or standing upright in dining-

Dishes

room hutches. We have found that brass and pewter buttons fill this need quite nicely. Most stores that carry material also have a box of loose buttons. Find the ones that attach from the back and have no hole in the middle. Remove the shank on the back with a pair of pliers. Pound the buttons into the shape of a plate with a hammer and you're ready for dinner. Larger buttons may be used for trays and fancy ones may be used for brass wall plaques.

PLACE MAT, CLOTH NAPKIN, GOBLET, AND SALT AND PEPPER SHAKERS

Civilized families need table coverings and miniature renditions are no exceptions. Individual place mats are the current rage in decorating and this one is made of small-checked gingham. Start with a piece 1¾-inches wide by 1¼-inches high. Sew a seam ¼-inch from each of the side edges. For the tassled edge, pull the cross-threads on the outside of the seam. The napkin is made from a piece of gingham, one-inch

Front of the house

Back of the house

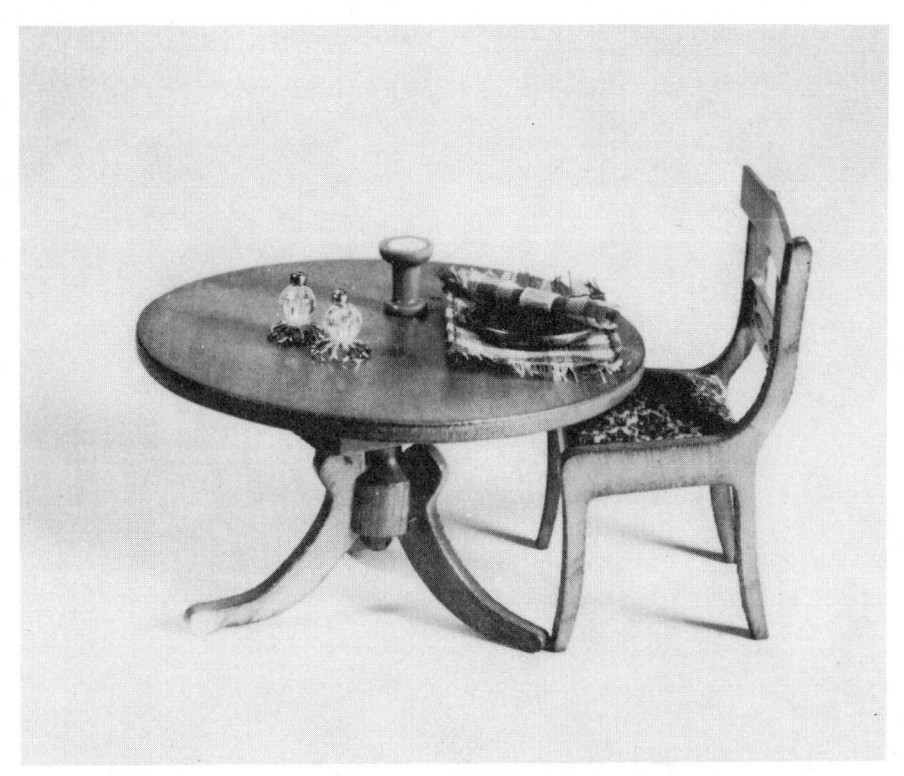

Place Mat, Cloth Napkin, Goblet, and Salt and Pepper Shakers

square, which was rolled by twisting it around a toothpick. For the napkin ring, use the cut tip of a plastic, colored straw. The goblet is a colored pushpin. The pin was pulled out with a pair of pliers (save this for the pen in your desk set) and the hole was filled in with glue. The center was painted white to look as if there was milk in the goblet. For the salt and pepper shakers, you will need two bead caps for the bottoms, two crystal beads for the middle, and two smaller beads for the top. All of these may be purchased in a craft or hobby shop. We painted our beads on the top a gold color to match the bead-cap bottoms.

BRASS COOKIE SERVER AND FLOWER VASE

These brass items will grace any dining table, whether it's a formal party or a family celebration. The cookie server is made from hollow-bottomed buttons in three graduated sizes. To cut down on the cost, ask your local dry cleaners if he will allow you to rummage through his lost button drawers. The cost will then be minimal, if anything. Using 3/8-

Brass Cookie Server and Flower Vase

inch lengths of a 3/16-inch wide strip of balsa wood, glue the first piece of balsa into the middle of the underside of the largest button. When this is dry, glue the medium-sized button, face down, on top of this connector piece of balsa. Continue with the other piece of balsa wood and the smallest button, completing the tiers. For the flower vase, use a brass bullet case and small flowers, either dried miniatures or plastic ones from a gift shop.

FLOWER BOWL AND CANDLESTICKS

When not in use for dining, tables need decoration. This flower bowl started out as a plastic suction cup found in hobby shops. Glue a small piece of florist's foam into the bowl and insert tiny, plastic flowers, dipping the tips of the stems in glue to keep them in place. The doily beneath the bowl was a design cut from a regular-sized paper doily. For the candlesticks, use a bead cap as a base and two crystal beads for the

Flower Bowl and Candlesticks

Square Tablecloth

body. These may be different colors. The "candle" is a white, narrow bead that has been glued into place.

SQUARE TABLECLOTH

If you have a square tablecloth or need one for the picnic table that is described in chapter 7, you can use another piece of the material used for the place mat. For a tablecloth, you will need a piece of material the size of the table plus 1-1/2 inches all around. Sew a double seam one-half inch from the edge of the cloth and pull the cross threads to make a tassle and you're ready to set the table. If you use a plain material, you may embroider a design around the edge of the cloth or a monogram in each corner.

COVERED CANDY DISH

A covered candy dish is another possibility for a centerpiece, if you can keep your dollhouse children from snitching samples. Our "crystal" dish was made from two suction cups. The bottom one had a flat base, while the top one was knobbed. Tiny beads or actual candy nonpareils can serve as the candy in the bowl that sits on another design cut from a paper doily. This lid may also be used as a cheese-dish cover over a flat plate.

NOODLEBOARD AND ROLLING PIN

Tables are also used for support when industrious mothers roll out the dough for cookies or homemade noodles. This noodleboard was a piece of 3/16-inch balsa, cut to a piece 2-inches long by 1-1/2-inches wide. The edges were made from 1/4-inch-wide by 1/16-inch-thick strips cut to fit the edges. The strips are glued to opposite sides of the board. The rolling pin is made from a 1/4-inch-diameter dowel. Cut a piece 1-1/2-inches long, attach a long, white bead to each end with a small nail for the handles, and your mother is ready to roll the dough into shape.

Covered Candy Dish

Noodleboard and Rolling Pin

Boxed Food

BOXED FOOD

Many foods come in boxed and frozen containers and these are simple enough to make in a miniature version. Find pictures in the right scale (1 inch to 1 foot) in magazine ads. Glue these pictures to balsa wood that is 3/16-inch thick. When dry, cut out the squares and paint the boxes the dominant color of the picture. Do not varnish, for the pictures will smudge. Now your boxed goods will stand on shelves, tables, and even in the refrigerator.

3
Household Necessities

Every miniature household needs certain accessories to keep it running smoothly. These are not luxuries, but basics in everyday life. What child could do homework without a lamp and what Lilliputian mother could keep house without a feather duster and a broom? The father, too, must keep the grass under control with a lawn mower, and every family would oversleep without an alarm clock beside the bed. There is a calendar to let the family know what day it is and even a small fly swatter for shooing away those tiny pests. It simply would not be polite to give a family a bathroom without toilet paper or towels or even soap in its own little dish. And every holiday brings its own special needs to tiny homes. The fact is that every household, large or small, must have many accessories for daily living. For more ideas, think of your own family and the things they could not do without in your everyday routine.

If you collect only period miniatures, you may feel that you can skip this chapter; but the truth is, it takes very little to change some of these necessities into period pieces. The table lamp, for example, could easily become a Tiffany lamp by exchanging the bottle cap for a large rounded button that could be painted to look like Tiffany glass. The fireplace screen might be used in a French Provincial room if the horsehair screen was exchanged for a piece of fancy embroidery or tapestry. Many of the other things, such as calendars and holiday decorations, fit into any decor and any period.

Fly Swatter and Calendar

FLY SWATTER AND CALENDAR

Every kitchen and country store needs a fly swatter and calendar. Our fly swatter, used to swat microscopic flies, was made with a single piece of wire that comes with Fun Film kits in hobby shops. Any thin wire that is easy to bend will do. Bend the wire in half and fold one piece over another for the stem, leaving enough to form the swatter. Bend the wire around and twist the ends together to form a square at the end. For the swatter part, you can use a small piece of a stiff lining or a pipe screen found in drug stores. Glue the swatter into place and let dry. Cut away the excess netting and hang the fly swatter on a nail.

The calendar is another picture found in a magazine and glued to a piece of cardboard. A small piece of string was taped to the back, allowing it to be hung on a tiny nail.

BRASS LAMP

No dollhouse or miniature scene is complete without a lamp and this one is solid brass. The base is a brass finial from a real lamp. These come in all shapes and sizes and you can have many different types and sizes of lamps, according to their design. The lamp shade is the cap from a plastic bottle. Here again, the size of the cap will depend on the size of your finial and you can experiment with different-sized caps. To hold the cap in place, stuff it with tissue, leaving a hole in the middle for the top of the finial. Pour white glue into the hole and place the cap on top of the finial.

CHANDELIER

If your dollhouse does not have electric lights in the middle of the ceilings, you will want to dress up the main rooms with a chandelier. To make one that resembles crystal, cut two pieces of Fun Film wire into 4-inch lengths. Connect in the middle by winding one over the other a couple of times in this way: ⇒⊕⎯. Using long, small, gold beads, dip eight beads into glue, then string them along each of the four sides (thirty-two beads in all). Finish with a larger, crystal-colored, round bead to fit over the last gold one, and then a single, white bead for the candle. When all the beads are dry, cut another piece of wire 2-1/2-inches long and twist one end around the middle of the four prongs. String

Brass Lamp

Chandelier

three large and two small crystal beads onto this length; then finish off the chandelier with a plastic, crystal, star shape used for hanging mirrors (found in any glass shop). Twist the other end of the wire behind this piece to secure it, glue it to your ceiling, and twist the candles into an upright position.

ALARM CLOCK AND PORTABLE RADIO

Without an alarm, every miniature family would oversleep. Fathers, and sometimes mothers, would be late for work and children couldn't get ready for school on time. This clock is made from a balsa wood dowel 5/8 inch in diameter. Cut a piece 1/4-inch thick and find a clock face in a magazine to glue to the front. For the alarm button and the feet of the clock, use small beads, gluing one on top and two on the bottom. Paint the clock and beads gold or any color to complement the bedroom.

Portable radios find many uses in miniature households. They go on picnics with the teenagers and travel from room to room as various

Alarm Clock and Portable Radio

Broom and Feather Duster

members of the family find programs they want to listen to. Find a radio face in a magazine first, then cut a piece of 3/16-inch balsa wood to fit behind it. Ours was an inch wide and 1/2-inch high. For the antenna and handle, cut pieces of thin wire and insert into the top of the radio. The handle is an inverted u shape, while the antenna is a 1/2-inch length of wire.

BROOM AND FEATHER DUSTER

Even dollhouses need to be cleaned every so often and here are two of the necessities. Tape several feathers from an old goose-down pillow (or buy feathers in a hobby shop if you have to) to a small strip of balsa wood with masking tape. Paint the tape bright red.

Real plastic broomstraws were used for the broom. These were snipped from the bottom of our broom and taped to a piece of balsa wood 3/4 of an inch long, and 1/4 of an inch wide. Cut a small slit into the middle of the top of the balsa wood for the handle, insert the tip of a three-inch strip of balsa wood (1/8 of an inch wide) with a touch of glue, and your broom is ready for use.

Roll of Toilet Paper

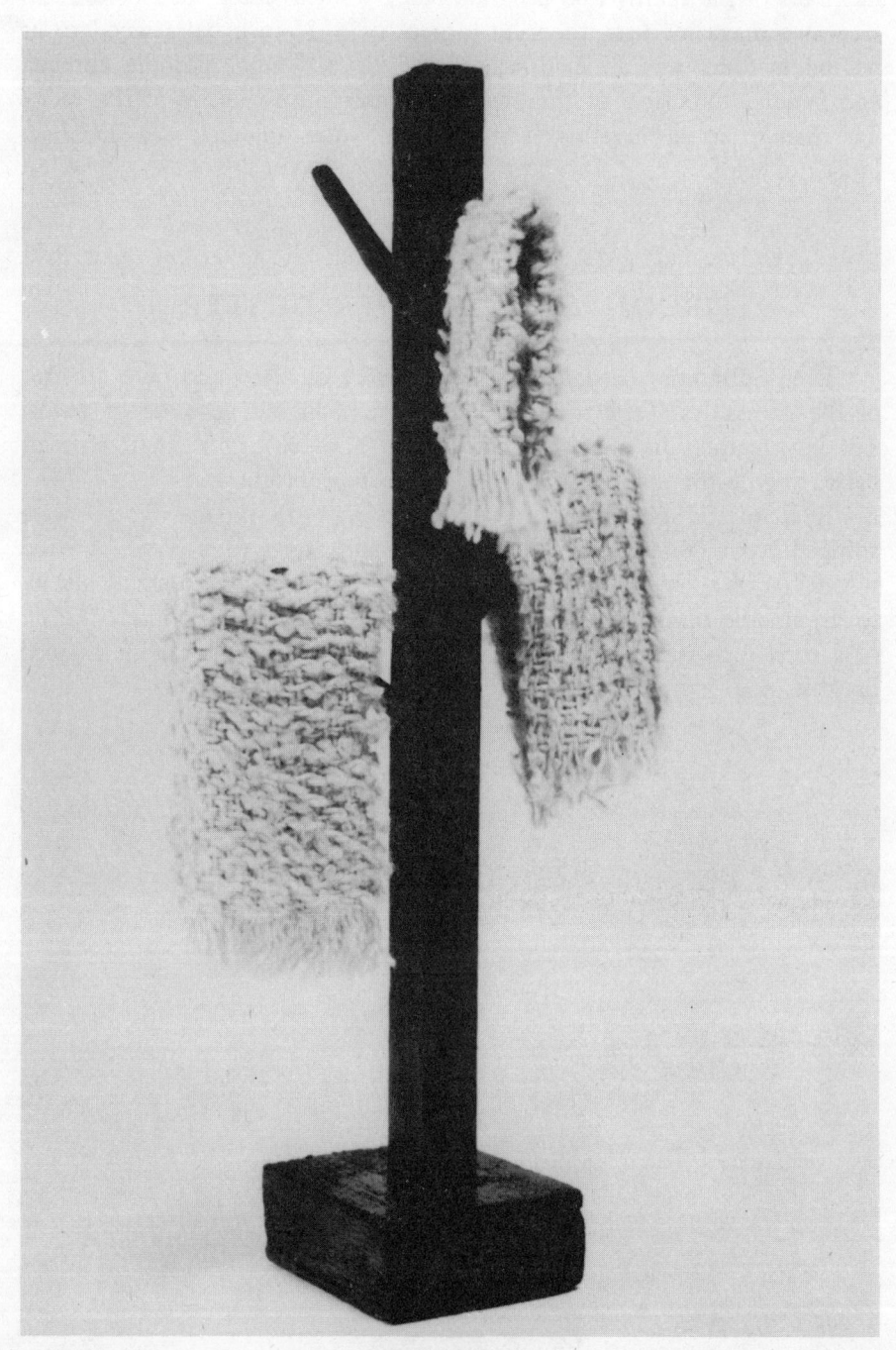

Towel Rack

ROLL OF TOILET PAPER

The considerate owner of any dollhouse makes sure that this necessity is always available. To make your roll of toilet paper, start with a push pin, found in packs in drug stores, and a small strip of real toilet paper. A lengthwise strip from a single square of paper will be sufficient. Put a drop of white glue on one end of the toilet paper and attach to the push pin. Roll up until only a little bit hangs down and put another drop of glue under the flap. Press into the wall beside the toilet and your dolls will surely thank you.

TOWEL RACK

What bathroom is complete without a towel rack hung with miniature towels for every member of the family? For the base, start with a 1-inch square piece of 3/8-inch thick balsa wood. For the post, cut a 4-1/4-inch length from a 1/4-inch square rod of balsa. Put this in the middle of the base and draw an outline around it with a pencil. Cut out this square in the base and, with a touch of glue, insert the post into the base. For the hangers, cut 3/4 to 1-inch lengths of balsa wood or use toothpicks. Make holes in three sides of the post with the edge of a toothpick and glue the hangers into place. Paint the rack to complement your bathroom. For the towels, use slightly worn washcloths that are still nubby, but are also thin enough to bend easily. For the larger towels, cut pieces 3 inches by 2 inches. The hand towels were made from 2-1/2-inch by 1-inch wide rectangles. Pull the end threads to make a fringe on the two shorter edges, then fold the other two edges back to meet each other behind the towel. Tack together with thread and fold the towel in half, ironing to make it stay folded. Hang the towels on the rack.

SOAP, SOAP DISH, AND PLUNGER

It would not be very polite to furnish a bathroom for a miniature family and forget the soap! Ours is a tiny rectangle of balsa wood painted white. To keep it from slipping off the edge of the sink, use a dish made from a tiny shell painted gold.

For another kind of emergency, you can supply the bathroom with a plunger made from a rubber faucet washer and a 1-3/4-inch piece of balsa wood for the handle. Use a 3/16-inch square rod of balsa wood,

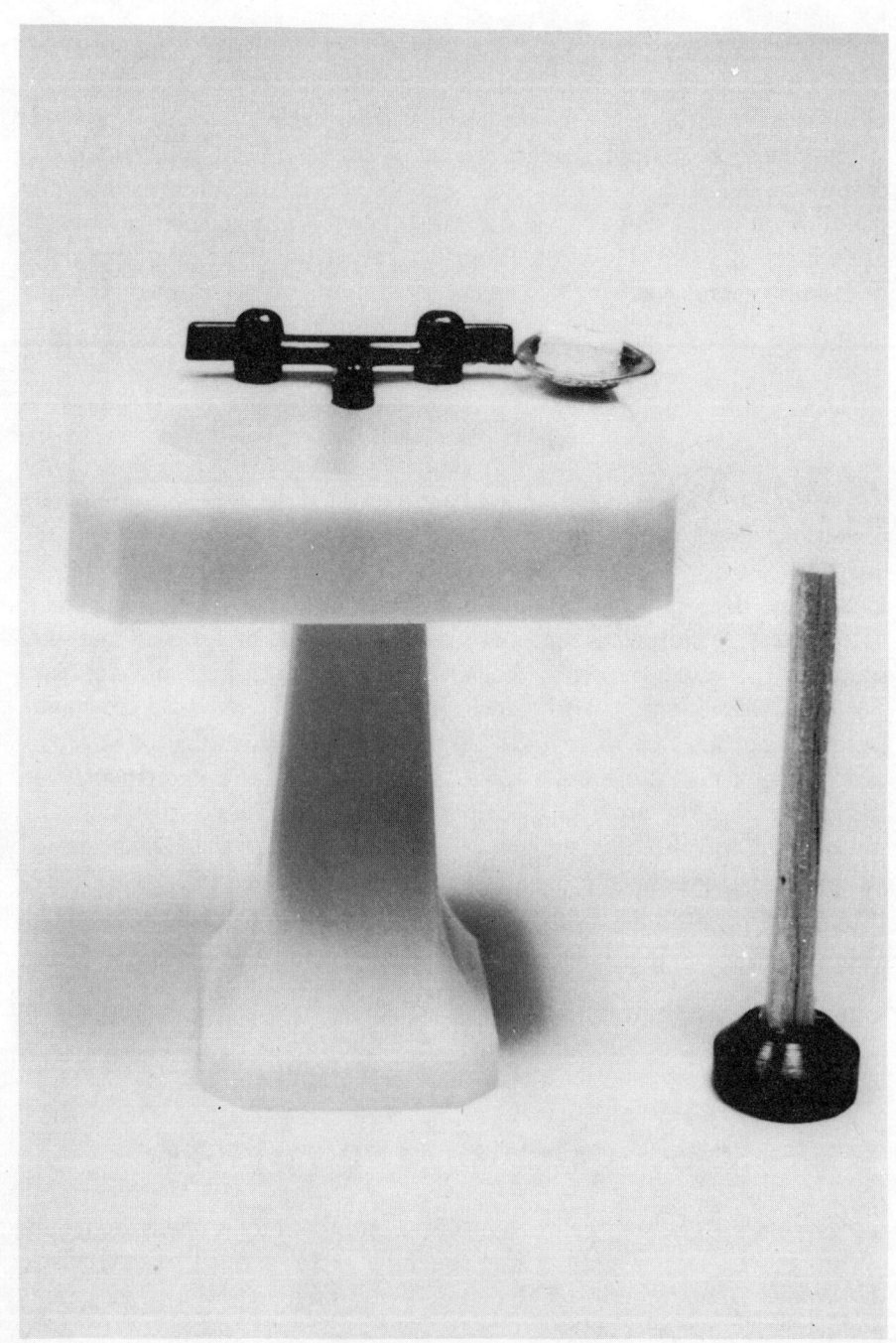

Soap, Soap Dish, and Plunger

Scales and Spice Cabinet

sanding it to a smooth roundness. Glue into the center of the washer, and your family will always be prepared.

SCALES AND SPICE CABINET

These two items have been put together because they both start from pieces of 3/16-inch thick balsa wood. For the scales, cut a piece 1-inch long by 3/4 of an inch wide. For the top, cut a piece 1/4 of an inch square. Glue the smaller piece to the top and sand the front edge to a rounded smoothness. Then sand the four corners of the bottom. Paint black and white as shown.

For the spice cabinet, cut two pieces of the 3/16-inch balsa wood. Cut one piece 3/4 of an inch wide by 1-inch high for the front, and another slightly larger piece, 3/4 of an inch by 1-1/2 inches, for the back. Glue the smaller piece to the larger one, matching the bottom and sides together. Cut rows of drawers into the top piece with an X-acto knife. Hammer tiny nails into the middle of each drawer as a pull.

Mailbox and Lawn Mower

Finally, sand the top of the bottom piece into a triangle and make a small hole for the nail to hang it on the kitchen wall. Paint yellow or any color that will complement your kitchen.

MAILBOX AND LAWN MOWER

Without a mailbox, even miniature letters would get lost, and how can a family keep their lawn looking neat without a reliable lawn mower? For the mailbox, use 1/4-inch thick balsa wood. Cut a piece 1/2-inch high by 1-1/4-inches wide. Cut the piece on the diagonal from each side to a peak in the middle, creating a triangular shape as viewed from the side. For the lid, use 1/8-inch balsa, cutting a piece 3/8 of an inch high by 1-1/4-inches wide and glue to the top. Paint the mailbox black with a small design in white on the lower half. For the newspaper holder, use a u-shaped piece of wire, inserting the ends into the bottom of the mailbox and folding up to cradle the newspaper, which was found in an ad in a magazine.

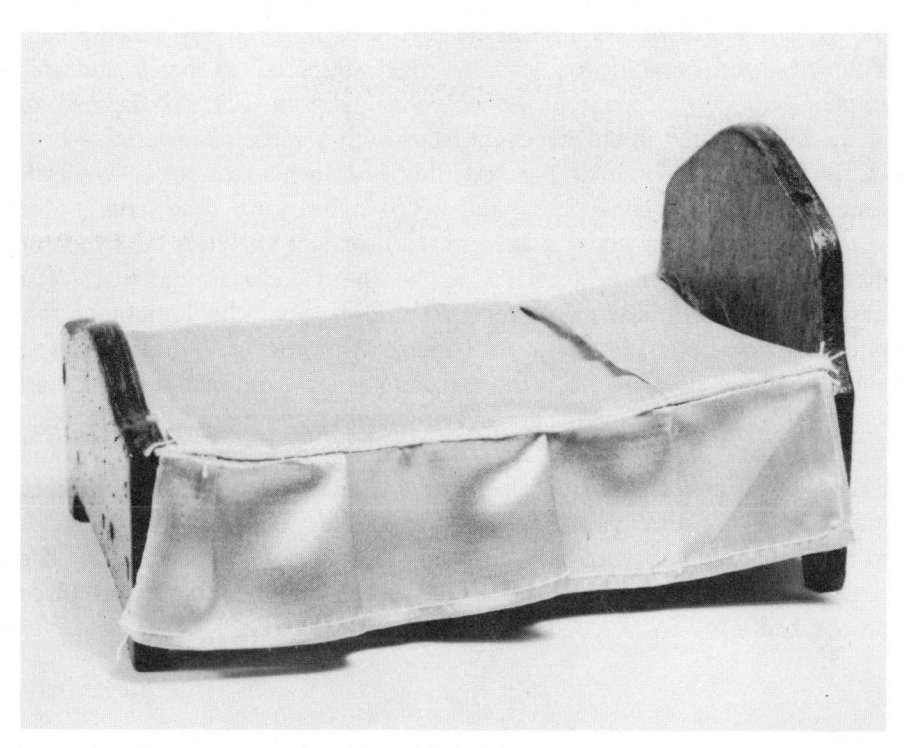

Bedspread

For the lawn mower, you will need two buttons, 3/4 of an inch in diameter, with four holes in the middle of each one. Using a flexible wire, string it back and forth between the holes in the buttons, leaving 1-1/4 inches between them. Finish off by taking the two ends over the top of each button and securing them in the middle of an 1/8-inch-thick piece of balsa wood, cut to a length of 2-1/2 inches. For the handle, cut a piece of the 1/8-inch balsa into a piece 5/8 of an inch long. Glue to the top of the length of balsa. To make sure your lawn mower keeps its shape, glue two pieces of balsa wood, cut to 1-1/4-inches wide, between the two button wheels; and paint the whole mower black.

BEDSPREAD

Great care is taken in choosing a regular-sized bedspread and the same care should go into choosing a bedspread for a dollhouse. Do you want to have it match the draperies? Should it be a rich, plain material or does the room need color with a patterned spread? Whichever you choose, one-fourth of a yard will be plenty of material for a bedspread. You will need more if you want to make draperies to match and this amount will depend on the size of your windows. For a bedspread to fit the bed pictured in chapter eight, start with a piece of material 4-1/4-inches wide (the width of the bed plus 1/2 inch extra for a 1/4-inch seam allowance on both sides) and 6-3/4-inches long (the length plus 1-3/4 inches). Turn under a hem or 1/4 inch at the head and foot of the bedspread. Fold over 1 inch along the head and sew into place. Fill this part with a folded tissue for the pillows. Fold the bottom of this pillow section back 1/4 of an inch to make it seem as if it was tucked under. For the sides of the bedspread, cut two pieces, each 1-3/4-inches wide by 7-1/2-inches long. Sew a 1/4-inch hem along the bottom edge and two sides of each piece. Finally, with the right sides together and using a 1/4-inch seam allowance, sew the sides to the middle part of the bedspread, gathering the sides to make it fit. Turn the material back to the right side and with the edges tucked under, sew a seam along the edge of the middle part of the spread. Iron for smoothness and place on the bed.

FIREPLACE SCREEN

If your dollhouse has a fireplace, it should also have a fireplace screen to ward off the imaginary sparks. This one is made from horsehair lining and balsa wood. Cut the horsehair into three pieces, a front piece 2-1/2-inches wide by 1-1/2-inches high, and two side pieces, each 1-1/2-inches high by 3/4 of an inch wide. Glue 1/8-inch wide strips of balsa wood all the way around the front piece and on one length and two widths of the side pieces. On the side pieces, make sure that the balsa wood extends to the edge of the horsehair. When dry, glue the three pieces together, bending the sides to fit the fireplace. Paint the balsa trim either gold or silver to match other fireplace accessories.

STANDING ASHTRAY

Even though smoking is no longer as popular as it used to be, ashtrays are still necessary. Smoking guests will usually look for one even if the immediate family does not smoke. This standing ashtray was made from two nuts and a dowel. Cut a quarter-inch dowel to a length of 1-3/4 inches. Glue the bottom into a square, quarter-inch nut. This forms the base. For the ashtray, glue a hexagonal nut to a piece of cardboard

Fireplace Screen

Standing Ashtray

Christmas-Tree Decorations and Stockings to Hang

and cut around the cardboard. Glue this to the top of the dowel. Paint everything black and make miniature pipes from bread dough.

CHRISTMAS-TREE DECORATIONS AND STOCKINGS TO HANG

Christmas is one of the best holidays for a dollhouse because the excitement of a young owner quickly spreads to the miniature family. A tree is a necessity and may be found in hobby shops that sell HO-scale accessories. This one is from the setting around the train set my husband had as a child, so you may also find them in antique shops. For decorations, string a long row of multicolored, different-shaped beads. Glue one end to the middle of the bottom of the tree and wind around and around until you get near the top and attach with glue again. Old strings of inexpensive pearls may also be used in this way and, if you are really ambitious, you may attach tiny charms in the shape of toys from gumball machines. For the stockings to hang by the chimney, cut out the stocking shapes from red felt (cut two if you want to fill them) and glue green trim to the top. Attach to the fireplace with double-edged tape and wait for an imaginary Santa.

CHRISTMAS PRESENTS

With a Christmas tree ready and waiting and the stockings hung by the fireplace, the only things missing are the presents beneath the tree. An easy way to make wrapped packages is to cover squares of balsa wood (1/4-inch thick at least) with regular wrapping paper. This is also a practical way to use up those scraps of balsa wood. For the ribbon, use paper that has adhesive on one side (colored tape will also work) and cut into small strips. Stick into place and make appropriate bows. Place beneath the Christmas tree and everyone will wonder at the contents of the tiny presents.

EASTER BASKET AND HALLOWEEN PUMPKIN

These are probably the two least original items in this book, since they are basically store-bought items changed to fit our needs. The tiny basket was bought in a local toy store and the rabbit was found at a flea

Christmas Presents

Easter Basket and Halloween Pumpkin

market, but could be made from Play-Doh. We used Play-Doh to fill the basket bottom, set the rabbit in the middle, then made Easter eggs from different-colored Play-Doh and glued them around the rabbit, making an adorable Easter surprise for dollhouse children.

For Halloween, a miniature pumpkin was found in the bakery shop in the shape of a toothpick novelty to stick into cupcakes. Simply break off the plastic-toothpick bottom and you have a pumpkin for the children to carry as a trick-or-treat bag or a decoration for the window when this holiday rolls around.

4
Window, Wall, and Floor Coverings

The Colleen Moore dollhouse at the Museum of Science and Industry in Chicago probably has the most beautiful walls and floors of any dollhouse in the United States. In the library, there is an undersea motif. The walls are painted to resemble the ocean, blending into the sky near the ceiling, which has a dome depicting the constellations. The inlaid-walnut floor is imbedded with golden signs of the Zodiac. In the drawing room, a rose-quartz floor is bordered in green jade. The walls are painted with murals and the stairway pillars are carved with motifs from fairytales. The floor in the bedroom of the princess was made from mother-of-pearl, bordered in gold, and fairy-tale motifs are painted on the walls and ceiling.

Such decorations are magnificent but they are not for the average dollhouse, especially if a child is going to be playing with it. For this, we need more practical decorations, reasonable in cost and fairly durable.

Instead of the stained-glass and cut-glass windows in the Moore dollhouse, most dollhouses have real glass or heavy plastic for windows. These need drapes and curtains. Your fabrics will vary with the style of the house and the effect you wish to give in each room. Velvet and satin should be used for formal rooms and period houses, while simpler fabrics with modern designs may be used for more contemporary houses.

Linoleum may be used for covering floors, as well as contact paper, with appropriate patterns. If you have good, wooden floors, you may wish to refinish them and use only area rugs, or you may want to go along with the current trend to carpet all the rooms. For this, you have your choice of many types of carpeting. If you have plastic furniture that is lighter than wood, you should choose a thinner, flatter carpet in the indoor-outdoor variety. You might also prefer to make Oriental carpets from material, as illustrated. If you have heavy, wooden furniture, you have a choice of the thinner carpets or the plusher materials found in carpet samples.

For the walls, I agree with Colleen Moore who claims that height must be overscaled to produce the illusion of reality. If you are making a dollhouse, make your walls higher than the standard eight feet (eight inches). To wallpaper dollhouse walls, there is a choice of contact paper, better-grade wrapping paper, or regular wallpaper, scaled to a miniature pattern, which is available from outlets that deal in miniatures. You can use diluted white glue or regular wallpaper paste available in paint stores. Wainscoting and chair rails add a finished touch.

Picking the right combination for your rooms will take some thought, but if you make a mistake, there is always the consolation of knowing it won't be as much work to repair as a full-sized room.

CAFE CURTAINS

A kitchen needs something bright and airy to give it a look of cleanliness and what could be better than lace cafe curtains? For these curtains, use the extra-wide lace for the bottom panel. This type comes with a scalloped hemline. For the valance, use a narrower piece of lace. To hang, measure the width of your window and add a half inch. Using this measurement as your length, cut two pieces from cardboard that you have cut into 1/4-inch wide strips. Sew the materials to these pieces, turning under the edges. Attach to your wall, using two-sided tape on the back of the cardboard.

BATHROOM CURTAINS

Bathrooms are pretty standard in most dollhouses and they can stand a little brightening with fancy curtains. These were made from embroidered ribbon bought in a store that sold material. Measure your

Cafe Curtains

Bathroom Curtains

Bedroom Draperies

windows and cut an inverted u shape of cardboard one-inch wide to fit the window. Glue two strips of the ribbon material to each side, letting it come down past the window 1/2 inch. This should be unravelled for a fringe. Finish off the curtains by gluing a piece of the ribbon across the top and gluing the ends to the back. Attach to the wall with two-sided tape.

We used this same method with red velvet ribbon for the living room, although we let the ribbon go down to the floor, making it look more formal. You may also add tiebacks if you prefer.

BEDROOM DRAPERIES

Bedroom draperies are often chosen to match the bedspread. Like our bedspread, these draperies were made of satin. They also started with an inverted u-shaped piece of cardboard an inch wide that was cut to fit around the window. For the sides, you will need two pieces the full width of the top of the u. Hem one length, and the bottom. Sew the other length of this material to the outside of one of the sides of the cardboard, matching the wrong side of the material to the underside of the cardboard. Fold over the material so that the right side is now on the front of the cardboard and iron four pleats into the material so that the hemmed side is just barely over the inner edge of the cardboard. Sew into place on the top of the u. Do the same for the other side.

For the top, cut a piece of material one-inch wider than the top of the u and one-inch longer. Using a 1/2-inch seam, sew the material to the wrong side of the top, once again matching the right side of the fabric to the wrong side of the cardboard. Then fold over the material and bring it down over the tops of the drapery sides and turn under 1/2 inch. Sew along the edge. Turn the sides of the material under the cardboard and sew along these edges as well. Attach to the wall with two-sided tape. If your pleats will not stay down, you might have to sew them into place with tiny stitches along the bottom.

CARPETING AND WALLPAPER

If you do not have neatly planked floors, you should probably consider carpeting your rooms wall to wall. For our rooms, we chose carpet samples that were being sold because of discontinued lines. If you choose this method, look for samples with bound edges. Cut the samples to fit your rooms and tack into place at the four corners. If your furniture is

Carpeting and Wallpaper

Wainscoting and Chair Rail

Bedroom showing draperies, bedspread, dresser and mirror, bed, nightstand, bullet flower vase, alarm clock, bookshelf

Study area showing desk set, trash can, and room divider

Front porch showing picket fence, porch swing, mailbox, bird feeder

Children's room showing bedspreads, TV, music stand

Kitchen showing stove, sink, refrigerator, calendar, bird cage, cafe curtains, wallpaper

Living room showing fireplace, screen, self-portrait, sofa, coffee table, magazine holder, standing ashtray

Shingled Roof

view, you might consider making a room divider like this one. Start with a piece of aluminum caning, available at hardware stores, and use tin snips to cut three equally long pieces. The height will depend on your need. Using 1/4-inch square pieces of balsa wood, cut four pieces the length of your caning. With an X-acto knife, make slits in the sides of the balsa wood (two in the middle ones, one for each end piece) and slide the caning into them after you have coated the edges with glue. Let dry and paint gold. This type of screen is well suited for a dollhouse because it lets a lot of light through it, but you may also wish to make other screens using Japanese pictures pasted to cardboard instead of the caning; and if you are talented with a needle, you could also make an original petit-point screen.

SHINGLED ROOF

Most dollhouse roofs have been neglected by the manufacturers. They are usually flat, textureless, and painted a single color. To make your

Oriental Area Rugs

Room Divider

roof more realistic looking, shingle it with sandpaper. Since the rows should have some order to them, cut the sandpaper into one-inch widths on a paper cutter if you have access to one. They may also be cut with scissors, but the job is more difficult. With white chalk, and a ruler, mark the strips at every inch and make slits no more than 1/2-inch deep. Attach the pieces of sandpaper to your roof with a large stapler. Start at the bottom with an uncut piece so that the color of your original roof will not show through. Stagger the rows so that the slits in every other row fall in the middle of each space. When you are finished, every other row should form a vertical line. For the peaked-roof lines, cut plain pieces, fold in half, and glue into place with epoxy.

5
Accessories for the Cultured Family

Any little girl or grown woman who has ever played with a dollhouse can tell you that miniature families are the brightest, most creative, most cultured people around. As reflections of what we would like to be, they read more than their human counterparts, they are more musically talented, and they are able to produce masterpieces in the arts without a single lesson. Depending on what the child-owner is used to, families may visit museums and art shows and even concerts, only to come home to produce their own versions of what they have experienced.

But the items on the following pages do not have to be used to reproduce masterworks. The music stand, for example, may hold the children's weekly music lessons as well as the mother's arias. The easel may be used in the children's play room for creative drawings as well as the latest art work of an adult, or a newly acquired painting. There are books for the nursery and the nightly story hour as well as classics for the adult bookshelf. And everyone enjoys reading magazines, whether it's *Humpty Dumpty* for the children or *Time* for the adults. A desk set is used for many things, from writing short stories to the weekly letter to grandparents telling of the interesting goings-on about the house. It's all here, to inspire variety and creative ingenuity in the dollhouse owner, who may then extend it to the miniature family.

Magazines and Newspapers

MAGAZINES AND NEWSPAPERS

Most dollhouse people are speed-readers and therefore need a lot of magazines to occupy their time. Ours were covers found in magazine ads. You have to find the ones in which the cover picture is complete; that is, it doesn't have another overlapping it. Glue these pictures to pieces of cardboard and display on coffee tables or bedside stands.

Our newspaper was also found in a magazine ad and unfortunately only pictured the top half. These pictures may be folded, delivery style, and left on front porches to show that the paper boy is on the job.

MAGAZINE HOLDER

After you have spread magazines about the dollhouse on coffee tables and night stands, you may find that you still have a small supply. For these, you need a magazine holder to put beside a favorite living-room chair. This one started as a square box made by gluing two pieces of balsa wood, 1-inch high by 1-1/2-inches wide to two side pieces, each

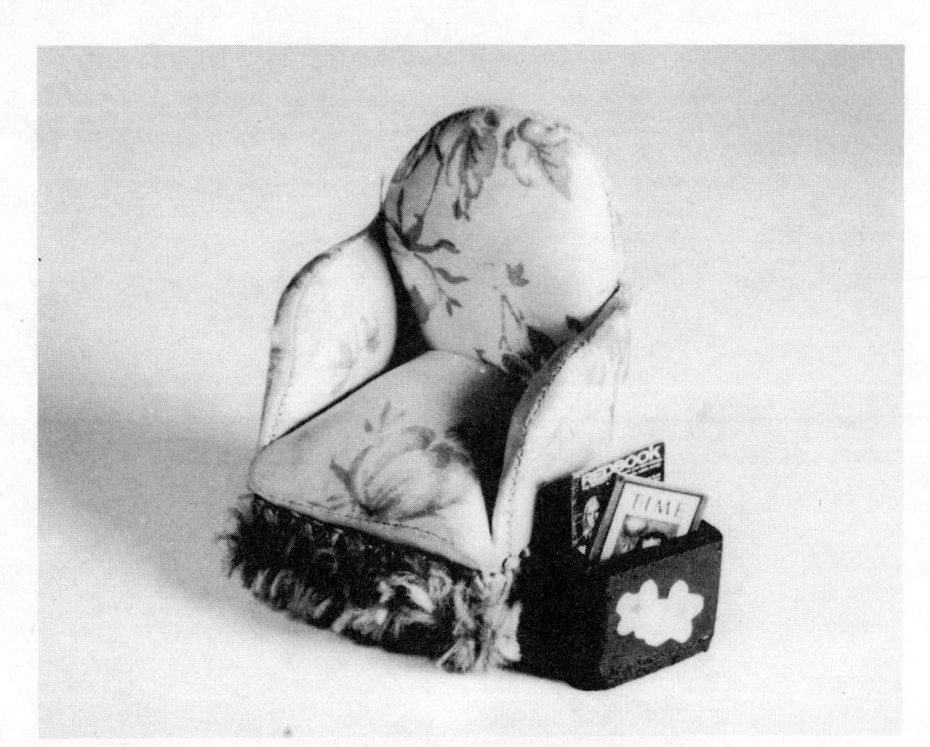

Magazine Holder

Children's Books

1-inch high by 1/2-inch wide. Glue this box shape to a base 1-1/4-inches long by 7/8 of an inch wide. When dry, sand the four edges to a rounded smoothness and paint the magazine holder. Small designs may be cut from magazines and glued to the front when the paint is dry.

CHILDREN'S BOOKS

Not only the adults need reading material in smaller-than-lifesized worlds. Dollhouse children also like to have books scattered about the nursery or placed neatly on bookshelves. These books are all-time favorites, sure to please the fussiest child, and they were found on the pages of Christmas toy catalogues from major companies. Once again, you have to be careful to find complete covers without numbers that overlap or pieces of other books cutting into the corners. Simply cut out the pictures and glue to a sheet of stiff cardboard. When dry, cut into individual books and leave in convenient places, remembering the bedside table where the considerate mother can find it to read at bedtime.

Paintings

PAINTINGS

You become the art connoisseur when you decorate a miniature room. There are many tiny pictures to be found in catalogues and the paintings are limited only by your taste. These pictures look as if they are framed already and need only to be glued to cardboard. They may form groupings on the walls, with the help of mounting squares that have adhesive on both sides, and may be cut to proper size.

FRAMES FOR PAINTINGS AND PORTRAITS

Some of the pictures and paintings found in magazines may not come with a framed border. For these, there are two types of framing that give a special effect in very little time. For the portraits, you can use a medium-weight aluminum foil found in craft shops. The major advantage of this foil is that it comes in many colors, including gold, which is the one chosen for these frames. Simply cut pieces to fit around your picture with scissors, then cut out the middle. Tape the picture to the back of the frame. If

Frames for Paintings and Portraits

Framed Self-Portrait

you wish, you may also decorate these frames with the point of a pencil, as we did in the oval one. For larger paintings, you can make a frame of balsa wood, using strips that are 3/16 of an inch wide. To make a perfect connecting edge between the pieces, lay one corner over another and slice through the middle of both with an X-acto knife, leaving both pieces with a diagonal match like this . Glue the four edges to the rim of the painting and either varnish for a natural finish or paint any color you wish.

FRAMED SELF-PORTRAIT

A sure way to please a young dollhouse owner is to give her a framed self-portrait for the living room or above the mantel. Formal pictures are best and we chose one from a slide taken at a recent wedding, but any colored print will do. Simply get a wallet-sized print of the colored picture and glue to a piece of stiff cardboard. We used a frame we had, but you can make a frame from pieces of balsa wood or colored foil as described under picture framing.

RECORDS

Most dollhouse families are lucky enough to own a record player, sometimes several, and this means they will need a large supply of records to choose from for their listening pleasure. Albums may be made by finding small pictures in magazine ads and gluing them to a stiff cardboard. You could also make records from circles of cardboard painted black and pierced in the middle to let them revolve on the turntable. By gluing only the edges of the album front to the cardboard back, these records may be placed inside their proper holder.

CHECKERBOARD

Dollhouse families need a lot of games since they have a lot more spare time than most people. A favorite with our family is this miniature checkerboard table. The table is an empty spool, painted with enamel paint. The checkerboard was a picture found in a catalogue and glued to a piece of cardboard, which was then glued onto the spool. The checkers are small black and red beads found in our local hobby shop.

Records

Checkerboard

Desk Set

DESK SET

There are so many reasons for having a desk in a dollhouse. There are letters to be written to friends and relatives and bills to be paid by the member of the family who tries to balance the miniature budget. If the mother is also a professional, say a teacher or a writer, there are papers to be corrected and stories to be written. Father can always use a place to finish his work from the office. For desk accessories, you'll need a pen in its own inkwell and this one is made from the pin you took out of the push pin for the goblet. Glue this pin, point down, into a large crystal bead, that is then glued to a bead cap for the base. The letters are small, white sheets of paper folded back and glued to look like envelopes. The simulated addresses were written on by hand and the stamps were drawn on with fine-point, felt-tip pens.

The desk blotter is a piece of colored matting board, 2-inches wide by 1-1/4-inches deep, or simply cut your piece to fit your desk. The woodgrained edges were triangles of contact paper and a piece of the same was cut to fit the back. This same contact paper was used for the wastebasket, which is really a disposable plastic salt shaker, sold in packs in the grocery store. With the aid of our lamp, the desk is ready for use.

BOOKSHELF

A bookshelf is a necessity for anyone who owns books and most dollhouses have a large supply. This bookshelf serves a decorative purpose as well as a place for treasured boxes and special photos. The skeleton of the shelf is made from four pieces of a balsa wood strip (1/8 of an inch thick by 3/16 of an inch wide) cut into 2-1/4-inch lengths. Cut two small notches into two of the pieces 5/8 of an inch from the end. Place these two pieces vertically on a piece of paper so that there is 1-1/8 inches between them. Place a third piece of the balsa wood into the notches and glue into place for the top shelf. Do the same with the fourth piece of balsa wood 3/8 of an inch from the bottom of the two original pieces. Paint.

For the books, use different heights and widths of balsa wood, sand-

Bookshelf

ing the edges slightly, then gluing onto the bottom shelf next to one another. Paint the books different colors and paint on small, black lines for titles. For the boxes, use a half-inch width and a 7/8-inch width of thicker balsa wood (or glue together two of the 1/8-inch widths) for the thickness. Paint one gold, the other silver, and add black latches.

For the framed pictures, use a piece of thin balsa wood 3/4 of an inch wide by 3/8 of an inch high. Make a slit halfway through the back and fold slightly. Paint silver and find two photos small enough in magazines to glue into place. Glue the pictures to the shelf and your shelf is ready to perform both a utilitarian and a decorative purpose.

FOLDING EASEL

As you may have noticed, dollhouse families are extremely talented in all the arts, and painting is often a favorite pastime. For this easel, you will need three pieces of 3/8-inch square balsa strips cut to 2-3/4 inches each. Attach the three pieces by passing a nail through the top of

Folding Easel

Music Stand

all three. Fold the middle piece back to make your easel stand. For more stability, cut the lower edges of the balsa legs on the diagonal, leaving the front legs longer in the front and the middle leg longer in the back. For the shelf to hold the paintings or drawings, cut a 1/8-inch-thick strip of balsa into a 2-inch length. Gouge a narrow slit in each of the front legs 1 inch from the bottom and glue the shelf into place.

MUSIC STAND

Most dollhouse children start their music lessons at an early age, and for this they will need a stand to hold their music. The base of this one is a square, quarter-inch nut that is heavy enough to hold the stand erect. The center post is a quarter-inch dowel two-inches high. For the holder, use balsa wood 1/8 of an inch thick. For the part that holds the sheet of music, cut a piece 1-1/2-inches wide by 1-inch high. Glue a strip (1/4-inch wide) across the bottom. To hold this piece, make a base on the dowel 3/4 of an inch square. To the top of this, glue a piece of balsa wood 3/4 of an inch wide by 1/2-inch high. Glue the piece that holds the music onto this base at a slant and paint the whole stand black. The instruments were from gum machines, although we painted them gold to look more realistic.

6
Homes for Household Pets

Household pets have been making dollhouses more attractive for hundreds of years. There is a watchdog and a bird in a cage in a French dollhouse from Alsace, France, built in 1680. More recently, the four white rats, three cats, two rabbits, six dogs, one canary, and three goldfish in the Faith Bradford dollhouse at the Smithsonian Institution have been competing for attention with the more elaborate furnishings.

In filling your own miniature scene, there are many pets to choose from. Dogs and cats are the most popular and the variety of breeds and sizes is almost endless. With so many people who collect these animals in miniature, you can easily find whatever you need for your setting in anything from porcelain to plastic. Fish and birds are also popular additions to dollhouses and these need bowls and cages. Many dollhouse children also keep mice and rabbits in cages, either in their rooms or out in the yard, depending on the mother's permissiveness. If you are lucky enough to have a yard for your dollhouse, you may also want pet turtles sunning themselves on rocks and wide-eyed toads ready to spring from beneath a bush. There are wild birds as well, who prefer to perch on feeders or the rim of a bird house.

There are many places to find miniature pets for your scene. Five-and-dime stores sell plastic models made in Japan, while toy shops carry the more detailed (and more expensive) imports from Great Britain.

Small gift shops and import shops will often reveal a treasure carved in stone or formed in glass, while you'd be more likely to find metal and porcelain animals in antique shops. Hobby shops often carry miniature animals and birds in craft packets, while a drug store might produce a special find among the racks of party favors. With such a variety to choose from, it is best to consider the purpose of the pet. Will it help to fill a child's dollhouse and be moved quite often or will it enhance a setting serving the pleasure of an adult?

Whichever pet you choose, of whatever material, you will soon find that they need a shelter of some sort and the following chapter will supply directions for basic homes for household pets.

DOGHOUSE

Dogs are by far the most popular animal for a dollhouse, and as such, there should be a big demand for doghouses. For our version, you will need a strip of balsa wood 2-inches wide by 3/16 of an inch thick.

Doghouse

Bird Cage

Birdhouses

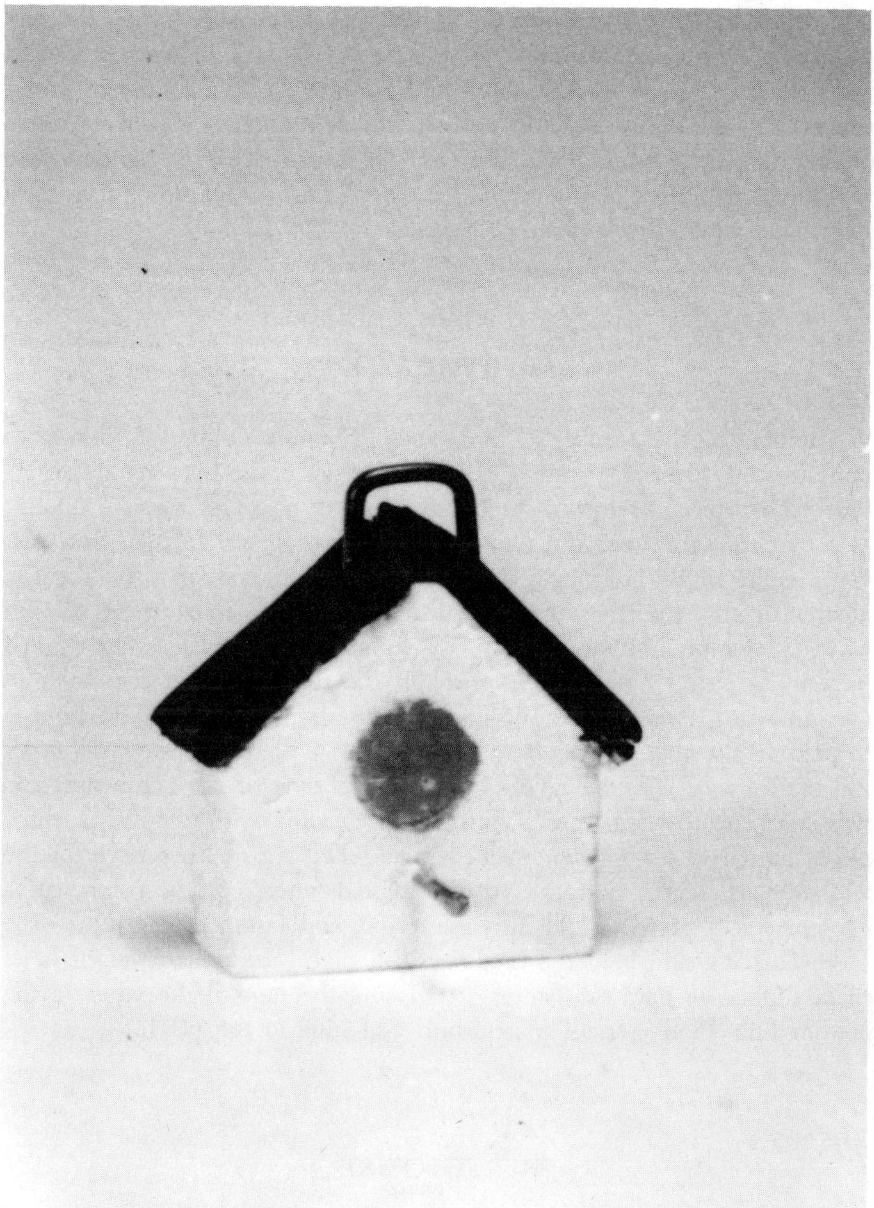

For the walls of the doghouse, you will need four pieces, each one 2-inches square. Cut a square hole in one of the pieces for the entrance. Then glue the four pieces together, overlapping the side pieces. To support the roof, cut two triangular pieces of balsa wood 2-3/8-inches wide at the base and 5/8 of an inch high at the point. Glue these to the front and back of the dollhouse. For the roof, cut two more 2-inch-square pieces of the same balsa wood. Glue the two pieces to the top of the doghouse to form a peaked roof and sand for smoothness. Paint and place in a convenient place beside your dollhouse.

BIRD CAGE

Judging by the number of bird cages in famous dollhouses, miniature families seem to have a special weakness for pet birds. For this bird cage, start with a piece of heavy cardboard. Cut out a circle, using a quarter as a pattern, and cover the top with a circle of green felt. With a pin, make eight small holes at equal distances from one another about a quarter of an inch from the rim of the circle. Cut four pieces of thin wire (preferably a brass color), which also bends easily, into 4-inch pieces. Pass one of these wires through the top of one of the holes in the cardboard, twisting the short edge beneath the cardboard to hold it in place. Take the long end, and fold into a u shape, passing the other end of the wire into the hole at the opposite side of the cardboard, and twisting beneath as before. Continue to do this with the other three pieces until you have an eight-sided cage. Then cut another circle of the felt and glue to the bottom over the twisted wires. For the perch, cut a two-inch piece of wire, fold into a u shape, and fasten to the top of the cage. To hang and hold the cage wires in place, use a lightweight brass chain (found in hardware stores), enclosing the tops of the wires in the bottom link. Find a small plastic bird and glue to the perch.

BIRDHOUSE

Not all birds like to be caged, and a birdhouse will draw many of the wilder, imaginary species. This one was made from balsa wood that came in a strip 1-inch wide by 3/8 of an inch thick. Cut a piece 1-inch square. Make the pointed top with an X-acto knife, starting 5/8 of an inch from the bottom on both sides and coming to a point in the middle. For the roof, cut pieces of 1/4-inch thick balsa wood into pieces 3/4 of an inch long by 1/2-inch wide. Glue to the top of the birdhouse. Paint the house white, the roof black, and a red circle for the hole. A small nail is used for the perch, while a staple nail is hammered into the roof for a hanger.

AQUARIUM

Some miniature families prefer goldfish, while others are fascinated with tropical species. Whatever they prefer, they are sure to need an aquarium. This one is made from the clear-plastic cover on a package holding a miniature car, but you can use the plastic cover of anything that has the right shape. Perhaps your pushpins or one of the other craft supplies we have been using came with such a cover. For the base of the aquarium, cut a piece of 1/16-inch-thick balsa wood to fit the bottom of the tank. Paint it silver and glue to the plastic. To make it more

Aquarium

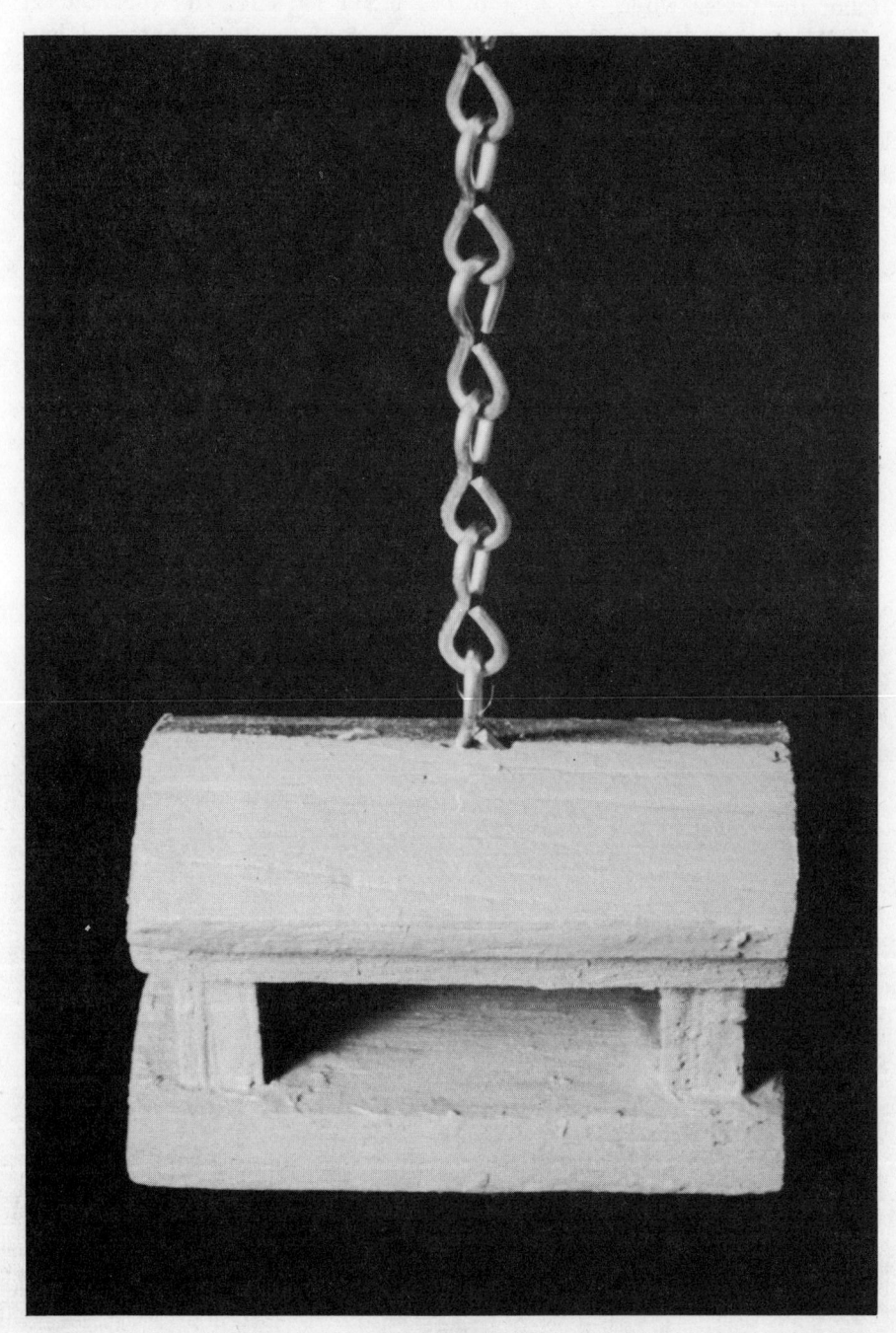

Bird Feeder

realistic, glue 1/16-inch strips along the four sides and also along the top of the tank. Paint these and the rim of the balsa base black to make it seem encased in metal. For the inside, use blue clay, molding a flat bottom, then taller columns for plants. Paint the plants green, leaving the bottom blue. Shape tiny fish from the clay, paint them gold or the colors of tropical fish, and glue them to the plants with white glue, letting the fish face different directions to give the effect of swimming.

BIRD FEEDER

If you have a front porch on your dollhouse, you might consider a bird feeder like this one. Cut two pieces of 3/8-inch-thick balsa wood into 1-1/2 by 3/4-inch pieces for the top and bottom. Cut two more pieces 1/2-inch wide by 3/8 of an inch high. Using the larger pieces as the top and bottom of the feeder, glue the smaller pieces between them for the sides. For the roof, use 1/4-inch-thick balsa wood, cutting

Rabbit Hutch

two pieces 1-1/2-inch wide. Cut a diagonal strip from one long edge of each piece. Glue the pieces together along this edge to form a peaked roof, then glue to the top of the feeder. Use the smallest chain available for hanging, and glue the bottom link into the middle of the feeder roof.

RABBIT HUTCH

A hutch such as this one may be used to hold any kind of wild pet, such as rabbits, turtles, raccoons, ducks, etc. Most of the cage is made from 1/4-inch-wide balsa strips (1/8-inch thick). For the sides, cut two pieces of a stiff netting into 2 by 1-1/2-inch pieces. Glue strips of the balsa wood onto the edges. For the end of the cage, cut two more pieces of the netting into 1-1/2 by 1-3/4-inch pieces. Glue the balsa wood strips around these edges as well and then glue a cross-strip on the one that will serve as the door. For the base of the cage, cut a piece of balsa wood 2-1/4-inches long by 1-3/8-inches wide. For the inner rim, glue 1-1/4-inch strips of 1/8-inch-thick balsa to the four lengthwise corners of the base; then glue four pieces around the top, forming a box. Next, glue the large sides of netting to this frame, then the end opposite the door. For a hinge on the door of the cage, glue half of a 1-inch-square piece of netting to the top of the door. Glue the other half to the top of the inner rim of the cage. Finish the top with five 2-inch-long strips of the 1/8-inch-thick balsa wood. The door will now open easily when the dollhouse children come to feed the pets or clean out the cage.

7
Outdoor Accessories

Many early dollhouses were furnished with elaborate courtyards. With "The Meierhof," a dollhouse made for Duke Philip of Pomerania about 1640, there was a walled courtyard with domestic animals roaming amid the cannon. There was a treelike pole used for games of the period and turreted towers overlooking it all. In the courtyard of the dollhouse of 1680 from Alsace, France, there is a poultry yard separated from the woodhouse, and an apiary for the bees. Most contemporary dollhouses do not go into much detail outside the house. A notable exception is the garden of the Brett house at the Museum of the City of New York. There is a floral setting behind their garden wall complete with an old couple having tea.

Most little girls do not appreciate such things, but I have found that they do enjoy recreating their own outdoor activities with their dolls. If your dollhouse is sitting on a platform, make a yard by covering it with green squares of rubber-backed carpeting, the flatter, the better. Cut the squares to fit around the house, glue into place, and you are ready to fill your yard.

For playing outside, dollhouse children will need a swing, sandbox, and even a climber. We found tricycles camoflaged as pencil sharpeners in our five-and-dime store and toys for the sandbox in gumball machines. A large jar lid may be painted and used for a wading pool, but most dollhouse dolls are not immersible.

There are outdoor activities to share with the adults as well, such as family picnics in the backyard with fresh vegetables in season and father barbequing on the outdoor grill. And who can forget those long, lazy afternoons spent chatting or just dreaming on the porch swing? There are shutters and flower boxes to beautify the outside of the house and even a picket fence to define the boundaries of the dollhouse property and to lend an aura of authenticity to the age of the building. It's all here, just waiting for you to follow the directions.

SWING

If polled, dollhouse children would probably select a swing as their favorite piece of gym equipment. This doll-sized one has a base of balsa wood 2-inches wide by 3-3/4-inches long. For the sides, use 1/4-inch-thick balsa strips. Cut two pieces, each six-inches long. With an X-acto knife, cut two squares (using the edge of the strips for a pattern) into the base 2 inches apart. Glue the posts into place. For the top piece, cut a strip 2-1/2-inches long and first glue, then nail onto the top of the posts. For the swing seat, cut a piece of the 1/4-inch balsa wood into a piece 1-1/2-inch wide by 1/2-inch deep. Make a hole in the seat about 1/8 of an inch from the edge. For the rope, use extra-strength thread or lightweight string. Cut a piece eleven-inches long. Make two small holes, one inch apart in the center of the top of the swing. Pass one end of the thread (you may want to use a needle) through one side of the seat, knotting it underneath; then pass it through the top of the swing and down through the other hole; and finally, pass it through the hole on the other side of the swing seat, knotting it underneath again. Paint the swing frame black and the seat brown or red.

SANDBOX

Any child can tell you that a sandbox is not a box of sand. It is a special place for digging tunnels and ditches and highways. You can cover things up with the sand or build great castles from your imagination. It is creative as well as useful, for it occupies children for hours and lets mothers of all sizes get their work done. For this miniature version, you will need a piece of balsa wood 5-inches long by 3-inches wide. For the sides, cut two pieces 5-inches long by 3/4 of an inch high and two other pieces 3-inches long by 3/4 of an inch high. Glue to the upper edge of the base to form a box shape. To secure the edges,

Swing

Sandbox

cut small, triangular pieces to fit the corners and glue onto the tops of the four edges. Paint the box and fill with sand or sawdust.

CLIMBER

A climber is useful for building young muscles and miniature children; if they are really like their young owners, they need this exercise as much as anyone. For this climber to complete your line of gym equipment, you will need four corner posts cut from 1/4-inch strips. Cut these four pieces 4-1/2-inches long each. For the crossbars, you will need eight 2-3/4-inch pieces of 1/8-inch-thick balsa wood. For the diagonal pieces, you will need four 3-inch pieces. Using two of the posts at a time, glue a 2-3/4-inch piece 1/2 inch from the top of each post. Glue another 2-3/4-inch piece 1/2 inch from the bottom. Do the same for the other two posts. Then glue two of the diagonal pieces into place. You now have two complete sides of the climber. Stand them up on end and glue the other two bottom pieces into place on the third and fourth sides,

Side of house showing picnic area with picnic benches and table, square tablecloth, food on table, picnic grill, rabbit hutch

Dining room showing grandfather clock, chair rail, cafe curtains, flower bowl, candlesticks, painting, wallpaper

Climber

Picnic Table and Benches

then the top pieces, and finally the diagonals. You should now have four complete sides. Paint it black and watch the children climb.

PICNIC TABLE AND BENCHES

Picnic tables are used for many things, from large family reunions to warm-weather birthday parties, when a lot of spills are anticipated. For this dollhouse-sized table, you will need a piece of balsa wood 6-inches long by 3-inches wide. Cut four 3-1/2-inch legs from a 3/16-inch strip of balsa wood. Cut the ends on the diagonal to make them stand flatter. Make the legs cross and glue them to the bottom of the table 1/2 inch from the narrow edge. Press a nail through the crossing point of the legs and, for a final bit of insurance against the legs coming apart, glue a 5-1/2-inch length of the balsa strip into the v made by the legs.

For each bench, use a 6-inch by 1-inch piece of the balsa wood for the seat. For the legs, cut two pieces 1-1/2-inches high by 1-inch wide

Picnic Grill

Hanging Planter

and glue these beneath the seat, one-half inch from each edge. To secure the leg, glue a small strip of balsa wood to the underside of the seat, next to each leg.

PICNIC GRILL

To complete your picnic ensemble, you will need a grill for pretend barbequing. This one started with the lid of an aspirin bottle that was then painted black. For the grill, glue the bottle cap face down onto a piece of netting. When the glue is dry, cut around the lid. To attach the legs, you will need a piece of balsa wood, one-inch square. Glue to the bottom of the lid. For the legs, use three 2-inch pieces of a 3/16-inch dowel. Cut three circles into the balsa wood and glue into place. Paint the legs and the piece of balsa wood black.

HANGING PLANTER

This planter may be used either inside or outside on a front porch. It is made from clay, the brown color that looks like pottery. From a ball of clay, form a deep, bowl shape, then pull the edges over to make a thick rim. For hanging, use the smallest, brass chain available in a hardware store. Make three 2-inch lengths and hook together at one end, with the bottom link of a 3-inch piece that will hang from the ceiling. To attach the chain to the pot, open the bottom links of the three lengths and hook into the top of the pot. Fill with small artificial ferns from a florist and you're ready to hang the planter.

WOOD PILE

Most dollhouses have a fireplace and a log pile beside the back door will be greatly appreciated on those cold winter evenings. This one is made from sticks, cut to a length to fit the fireplace and glued together with white glue to keep them from rolling about. The pile may be as big as you wish and you may also find a baby squirrel like this one in a gift shop or novelty department to dress up your wood pile. A miniature axe, like the plastic ones found in gumball machines, would be another possibility.

Wood Pile

Shutters

SHUTTERS

Shutters will dress up the outside of a dollhouse even if they are not the type that close. Measure your windows from the ends of the trim and use this width for the side of your shutters. Our windows, with their extra trim, measured four inches, making the two-inch-wide (3/16-inch thick) balsa wood perfect for the shutters. Add trim by gluing quarter-inch strips of balsa wood an inch from the edge of the shutter. Paint black and attach to the house with two small nails.

WINDOW BOXES

A flower box beneath a window on a house says many things about the owner. He or she is certainly a nature-lover and flowers rank high on the list of favorite plants. Flower boxes also spell neatness and orderliness, attributes which any member of a dollhouse would gladly claim. For this miniature flower box, measure the bottom width of your window.

Window Boxes

Using quarter-inch balsa wood, cut a 1/2-inch-wide piece the length of your window. Cut another piece for the front 3/4 of an inch wide (plus the length of your window). Cut two side pieces, each 1/4 of an inch wide by 3/4 of an inch high. Glue the front and sides on top of the bottom piece and let dry.

While this is drying, cut a piece of florist's oasis (a hard, green, plastic, foamlike substance) 1/4 of an inch thick and one-half-inch high and the length of your window minus half an inch. Glue into the window box. Paint the window box red and when dry, glue to the dollhouse, adding one nail to make sure it stays in place. Fill with tiny artificial flowers and greens that should be inserted directly into the foam.

PICKET FENCE

If you have a yard for your dollhouse, you might want to enclose it with a picket fence to separate the lawn from the sidewalk. It not

Picket Fence

Porch Swing

only helps to keep miniature toddlers in the yard, but makes the property look neater as well. For the posts, cut 3-inch lengths of quarter-inch-square balsa wood. Make 1/4-inch-long notches in the side of the posts 1 inch from the top and 1 inch from the bottom. You will only need these cuts on one side for end posts, but on opposite sides for the middle posts, and on connecting sides if your fence is going to turn. To support the pickets, cut 4-1/2-inch pieces from 1/4-inch-wide strips of balsa. Glue into the posts. The pickets are also cut from 1/4-inch-wide strips. Cut eleven pieces for each section, each piece 2-1/4-inches long. Cut one end of each to a point. Glue onto the horizontal bars. When dry, paint the fence white and glue into place on the perimeter of your lawn.

PORCH SWING

If you have a front porch on your dollhouse, you must make a porch swing. This piece is easily the most popular attraction of our dollhouse and I can practically guarantee its success on your front porch as well. For the seat, cut two 1-3/4-inch-long pieces of 1/4-inch-wide balsa strips. Cut six more pieces, each 5-inches long. Placing the two short pieces down in front of you vertically, glue the long pieces to them in a horizontal position. While this is drying, repeat the procedure for the back of the swing and glue into a vertical position behind the last seat rail. To make sure the back stays in place, glue another five-inch piece behind it.

For the arms, cut two pieces, each 1-1/2-inches long, and two more pieces each 1-1/4-inches long. Using the longer pieces for the arms, glue them between the third and fourth slats of the back of the swing. Glue the shorter pieces between the first and second slats of the seat, letting them support the arms. For the chain, use a small, brass chain cut to fit your porch. Use eye screws to attach it to the swing arms.

8
Furniture

The antique dollhouse of tomorrow will be the one that shows life as it is today. Among famous dollhouses of the past, the Uppark babyhouse in England shows life as it was in the early 1800s, right down to the mother who has just delivered twins at home. The Warren dollhouse, at the Essex Institute in Salem, Massachusetts, shows how an aristocratic Boston residence of the 1850s was furnished. Approaching our time, the Faith Bradford dollhouse occupies a prominent place in the Smithsonian because it shows the life of the large well-to-do Doll family living around 1905. A good way to let your own dollhouse have lasting value, therefore, is to fill it with furnishings and accessories that can artistically tell the story of today.

For your furnishings, you should choose a hard wood. Many of the books on the market today give directions for furniture made from cardboard. This looks beautiful but it will not last. The pieces on the following pages were made from a two-by-four-inch piece of pine cut to a length of two feet. Balsa wood was used for trim. The two-inch width of the pine was cut to 1-1/2 inches since 2 inches is a little too wide for most dollhouse furniture. Try to buy your piece of wood at a lumber mill, then ask them to cut it as follows:

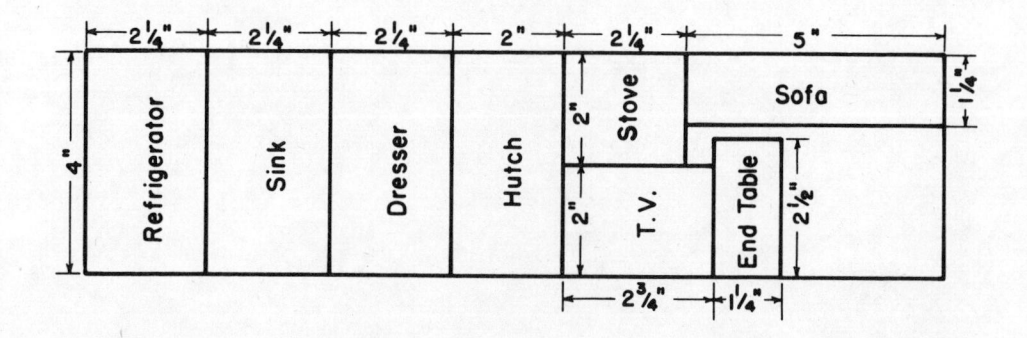

Although these furnishings are sturdy and will probably last several lifetimes if cared for properly, you do not have to be a carpenter to make them. Most of the things, once the pine was cut, were made with the help of a hammer, sandpaper, and an X-acto pen. A ruler and a ball-point pen were used for making drawers and old decorating magazines were hoarded for the items that needed pictures.

STOVE

Life would be rather dull without a stove in a dollhouse. There would be no way to make dinner, heat the baby's bottle, or bake the birthday cakes. To make this model, use the piece of wood you had cut to 2 inches by 2-1/4 inches. Set it upright so that the 2 inches is the width of the top and the 2-1/4 inches is the height. Glue a strip of 1/4-inch-wide balsa wood across the rear of the top. For the front door, cut a piece of 1/8-inch-thick balsa wood into a 1-5/8-inch square. Glue to the front and pound a small staple nail halfway in for the handle. Cut another piece of 3/16-inch-thick balsa wood 1-3/8-by-1-6/8-inches and paint this black. Paint the rest of the stove white, or any color of modern appliances. When dry, glue the black piece to the bottom. For the burners, cut pictures from ads in catalogues, along with the switches, and glue into place as shown. (The frying pan with the eggs was a charm from a gumball machine.)

REFRIGERATOR

Refrigeration has come a long way since the pioneers used fruit cellars and our grandparents used ice boxes. Today's refrigerator defrosts itself, holds more than ever before, and has become an attractive necessity in every kitchen. This refrigerator is made from the piece of wood you had

Stove

Refrigerator

Sink

cut to 2-1/4 inches (the width) by 4 inches (the height). For the door, use 3/16-inch-thick balsa wood and cut a piece 2-inches wide by 3-3/4-inches long. Glue to the front and paint this whole piece white, or a color to match the stove. Use a staple nail for the door handle. For the base of the refrigerator, cut a piece of the 3/16-inch-thick balsa wood into a piece 1-3/4 inches by 2 inches. Paint black and glue to the bottom.

SINK

Indoor plumbing made dishwashing a great deal easier for the modern housewife. To duplicate this appliance in miniature, use the piece you had cut to 4 inches (width) by 2-1/4 inches (height). For the top of the sink, you will need a piece of 3/16-inch-thick balsa wood cut to a piece 4-1/4-inches long by 1-5/8-inches wide. Carefully, using an X-acto knife, cut a hole out of the right side measuring 1-5/8-inches wide by 1-1/4-inches high. Glue this piece to the top of the sink and round off the edges with fine sandpaper. Paint the bottom of the sink white or a color to match the stove, and the top silver.

For the doors on the bottom of the cabinet, use a marking pen or a ball-point pen and make a rectangular shape (using a ruler) 3-1/2-inches wide by 1-3/4-inches high. Cut this in half at the 1-3/4-inch point. Use two staple nails for the handles, two large tacks for the hot and cold faucets, and a large staple nail with one end cut off with tin snips for the spigot.

TABLE AND CHAIR

There are several pieces of furniture that are indispensable to a dollhouse and a table and chair are two of them. For this table, use 3/8-inch-thick balsa wood for the top. Trace a pattern around the lid of a one-pound coffee can and cut out. Glue this table top to a ceiling adapter used for making spindle shelves. These are found in most hardware and department stores. Paint the entire table brown, or cover the top with wood-grained contact paper.

For a chair, start with a 3-1/2-inch by 1-1/2-inch piece of 3/8-inch-thick balsa wood. To make the legs, cut a one-inch square into the bottom of the piece. Round off the legs with sandpaper. Use the sandpaper on the top of the chair as well, until it forms a rounded, inverted v. Finally, gouge a 1-1/4-inch-wide hole (but do not go all the way through the chair) one-quarter-inch above the opening between the legs. Glue into this a seat that has been cut from the same balsa wood and is 1-1/4-inches wide at the back, but 1-1/2-inches wide at the front. For the front legs, cut a piece of balsa wood 1-1/2-inches wide by 1-1/4-inches high. Make legs on this piece as you did on the back piece, cutting a one-inch square from the bottom and sanding the legs. Glue this piece under the front part of the seat and let dry.

To make the chair fancier, cut an oval from red felt and glue to the front of the chair back. Cover the seat with red felt as well, and then cut a 3/8-inch strip to go around the side of the seat.

SOFA

There are wing-back sofas and pillow-back sofas. There are Chippendales and Queen Annes. There are high backs and tufted backs. There are many different styles of sofas, but this one is the simplest, yet most elegant one I could think of for a dollhouse. Take the piece of hard-

Table and Chair

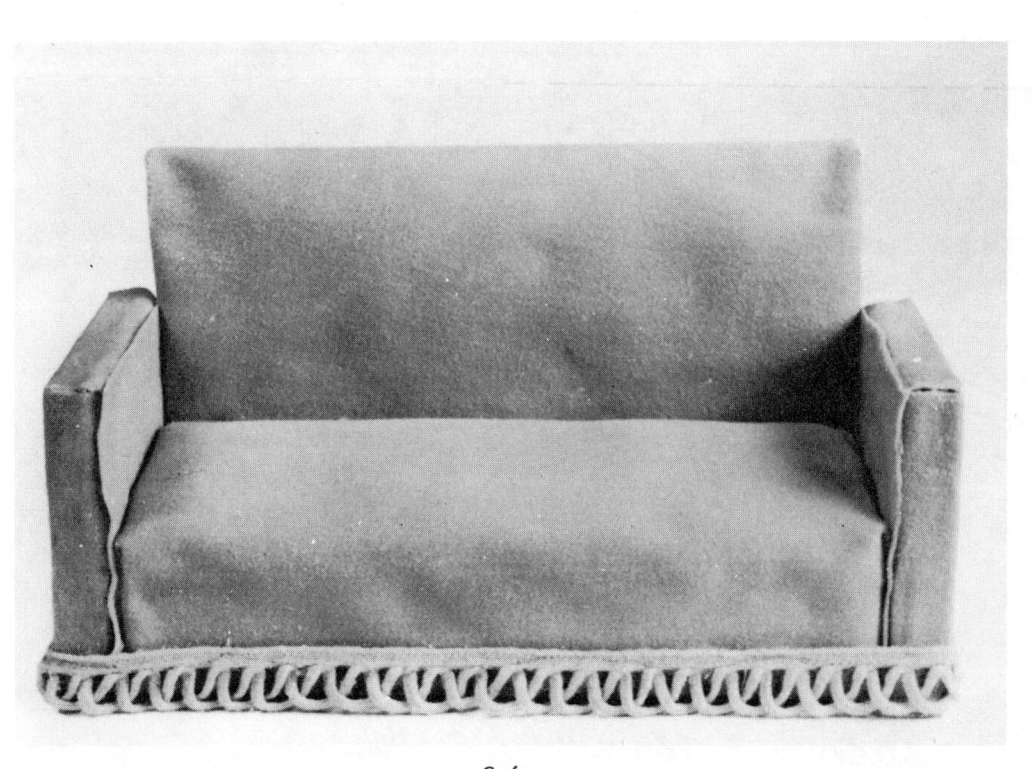

Sofa

wood that you had cut for a sofa base. Using the 5 inches as the length of the sofa, turn it so that the 1-1/4 inches becomes the height. Cover the top with cotton balls you glue into place (or you may use the cotton from medicine bottles as we did). Cover everything with a piece of red suede cloth, cut to measure 9-1/2-inches long by 5-inches wide, gluing the ends (about 1 inch all around) to the bottom of the wood. For the back, cut a piece of cardboard 5-inches long by 3-inches wide. Glue cotton to the upper half and cover the whole piece with the suede cloth, turning the edges under along the sides. Glue this piece, with the cotton on the upper half, to the back of the seat portion.

For the arms, cut two pieces of cardboard 2-inches high by 1-3/4-inches wide for each side. Glue 1/4-inch-thick strips of balsa wood around the edges of one of the cardboard pieces. Glue the other piece of cardboard on top of the balsa wood. Cover one side and three of the edges with the suede cloth, cutting the corners to fit, and glue to the outer side of the arm. Cover the inner side of the arm with a piece that fits it exactly. Nail the arm to the seat of the sofa with small tacks along the bottom. Repeat for the other arm on the other side. To hide the tacks, cover the bottom of the sofa with a decorative trim.

Dining-Room Hutch

DINING-ROOM HUTCH

A dining-room hutch serves several purposes. It stores treasured silver and table linens, and it also displays special dinnerware to best advantage. For this addition to your dollhouse dining room, take a piece of wood you had cut to a length of 4 inches and a height of 2 inches. Cut a piece of 1/8-inch-thick balsa wood into a 4-inch-square. Glue to the back of the base. For the top of the base, cut a piece of the same balsa wood 4-inches-wide by 1-5/8-inches deep. Glue to the top of the base. For the sides of the upper part, cut two pieces of balsa wood, each 1-inch wide by 2-inches long. Glue to the back of the hutch and round off the upper edge of each piece with sandpaper. For the shelf, cut a piece of balsa wood 5/8 of an inch wide by 3-3/4-inches long, and glue between the sides. To finish off the hutch, glue a 1/4-inch-wide strip across the top. Paint the entire hutch brown at this point. For the drawers, make an outline with a ball-point pen, using a ruler as a guide. Use tiny brass nails for the handles. For plates, find attractive brass or silver buttons. Remove the shank on the back with pliers. Hammer the buttons flat. Attach with two-sided tape.

COFFEE TABLE

A coffee table in front of a sofa can hold copies of magazines, an attractive flower arrangement, possibly a chess set, and very often, an ashtray with a cigarette lighter. This coffee table was made from a sample of paneling found in a lumber store. The samples are free and your only decision will be the type of wood you want. This sample came in a 2-3/4-inch length and I cut it to a width of 1-1/4 inches. To hold the legs, cut a piece of balsa wood 1-inch wide by 2-1/4-inches long. Cut a 1/4-inch-square piece from each of the four corners and glue the large piece to the bottom of the table top. Cut four 1-inch lengths of quarter-inch balsa wood for the legs and glue into the cut squares. Round off the legs with sandpaper. Paint or stain the bottom of the coffee table and you're ready to decorate it.

HASSOCK

Every working man or woman needs to put their feet up when they come home from their tiring job to relax with the newspaper. Here we

Coffee Table

have one just the right size for a dollhouse. Start with a small, round, unfinished pill box from a store that sells unfinished furniture. Cut a piece of red felt the width of your box and glue around the side. Place the box on the felt and draw around it for a pattern for the top. Cut out this felt and glue to the top of the box and your hassock is ready to do its job.

FIREPLACE

Fireplaces are used for decoration as well as heat, and this one will fit the decor of most dollhouses. Start with a base of balsa wood, 3/16 of an inch thick, cut to a length of 2-3/4 inches and a width of 1 inch. Glue onto this two threaded connectors, also used for making spindle shelves, and found in hardware stores. Cut a piece of balsa wood 1-1/2-inches wide by 1-1/4-inches high. Glue this between the connectors. Cut a mantel 3/4 of an inch wide by 3-1/4-inches long. Glue to the top. Paint the fireplace white.

Hassock

Fireplace

For the back of the fireplace, cut a piece of cardboard 2-1/2-inches wide by 3-inches high. Find a picture of a roaring fireplace in the right perspective in an old decorating magazine and glue to the base of the cardboard. Glue the cardboard to the back of the fireplace, covering the base, but not the back of the mantel. For decoration, you may glue a coat of arms (this one was originally an inexpensive pin) to the front of the fireplace.

TELEVISION

Any dollhouse that attempts to show life as it is today must contain a television set and this one even changes channels! Start with a piece of hardwood that was cut to 2 inches (height of TV) by 2-1/2 inches (width). Cut four pieces of quarter-inch-square balsa wood into 5/8-inch pieces. Glue to the bottom of the pine for the legs and round off by sanding. To secure more fully, hammer a long, thin nail through the middle of the leg and into the bottom of the set. For the front, cut a piece of 3/16-inch-thick balsa wood into a 2-inch by 2-1/2-inch piece. Starting 3/16 of an inch from the left side, cut out a square 1-5/8 inches by 1-5/8 inches. Carefully, cut away half of the back edge of the balsa wood on the side closest to the cut-out square. Glue the front of the television to the hardwood piece, making sure that you have an opening on the left side of the hole for the picture. Use two brass nails for the knobs on the lower right side and round off the top with sandpaper. Paint the whole set brown.

For different channels, cut pictures from the comics section of the newspaper, making them 1-5/8-inches high by 1-3/4-inches wide. Glue to a stiff cardboard and cut out. Change channels by sliding different pictures in and out of the left side of the television.

GRANDFATHER CLOCK

Grandfather clocks have long figured in nursery rhymes and fiction and this same fascination goes with them into a dollhouse. This clock

Television

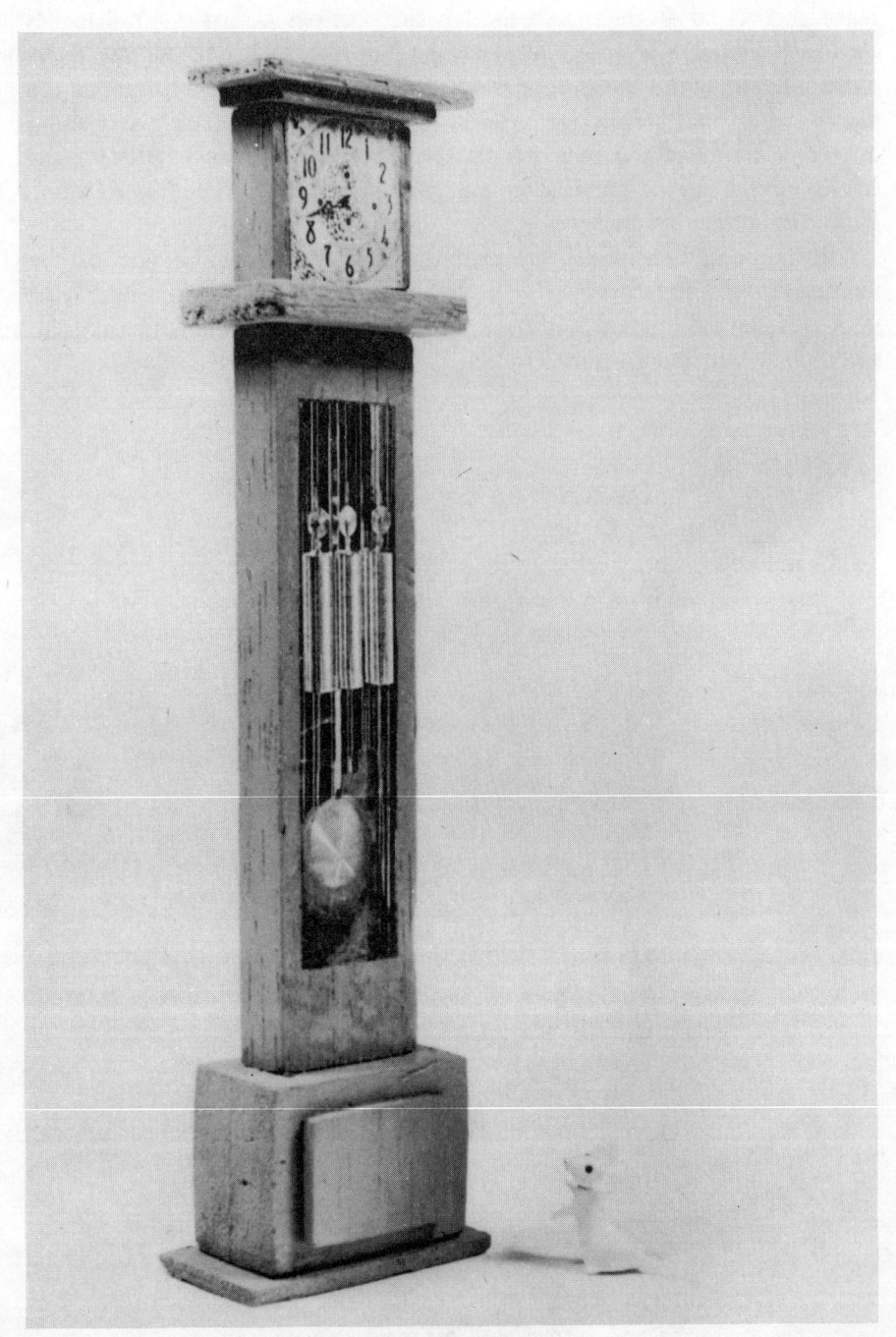

Grandfather Clock

was made from various thicknesses of balsa wood. The thick base for this one was cut from a 3/4-inch-thick piece of balsa wood that comes in one-inch widths. Cut a piece 1-3/8-inches long. This will be the width of the base on the clock. Glue this to a piece of 1/8-inch-thick balsa wood cut to 1-3/4-inches wide by 7/8-inches deep. For the middle, cut a piece of 3/8-inch-thick balsa wood (also 1-inch wide) 3-3/4-inches long. Glue to the top of the base. Cut the next piece from a piece of 3/16-inch-thick balsa and make it 7/8-inches deep by 1-3/8-inches wide. Glue on.

For the piece that will hold the clock face, use the 3/8-inch thickness you used for the middle piece and cut a 1-inch square. Glue onto the last piece. For the top, use the 1/8-thick balsa again and cut a piece 1-1/16-inches wide by 5/16 of an inch deep. Glue to the top, and on top of this glue another piece of the same thickness, but 1-1/2-inches wide by 3/4 of an inch deep. You may also wish to decorate the base of the clock with a piece of 1/8-inch-thick balsa cut to a width of 1-inch by 5/8 of an inch high. Glue to the bottom and paint the whole clock brown.

For the face of the clock and the chimes, look for old decorating magazines that have advertisements of grandfather clocks, cut the face and pendulum section to fit your clock, and glue into place.

BED AND NIGHTSTAND

A bed is certainly another one of the indispensables for a dollhouse. For this simple model, use balsa wood, 3/16 of an inch thick. For the headboard, cut a piece 4-inches wide by 3-1/2-inches high. For the legs, cut a piece 3-inches long by 1/2-inch wide from the bottom, leaving a 1/2-inch leg on either side. Sand the top of the headboard to a rounded smoothness. You may use 1/2 of a coffee can lid as a pattern. For the footboard, use a piece of the same width balsa wood 4-inches wide by 2-1/4-inches high. Cut out legs as before and sand as before. For the middle of the bed, cut a piece of wood 3-3/4-inches wide by 5-1/4-inches long. For the sides, cut two pieces, each 5-1/2-inches long by 3/4 of an inch wide.

To assemble, make four cuts, 3/4 of an inch long, 1/4 inch from each of the sides of the headboard and footboard, starting 3/8 of an inch from the bottom. Do not cut *through* the wood. Glue the sides of the bed into these cuts. When dry, glue the middle part of the bed onto these pieces, securing it between the headboard and footboard, and your bed is finished. Paint it brown. Gold decals may be added for decoration or you may wish to draw a design with a ball-point pen.

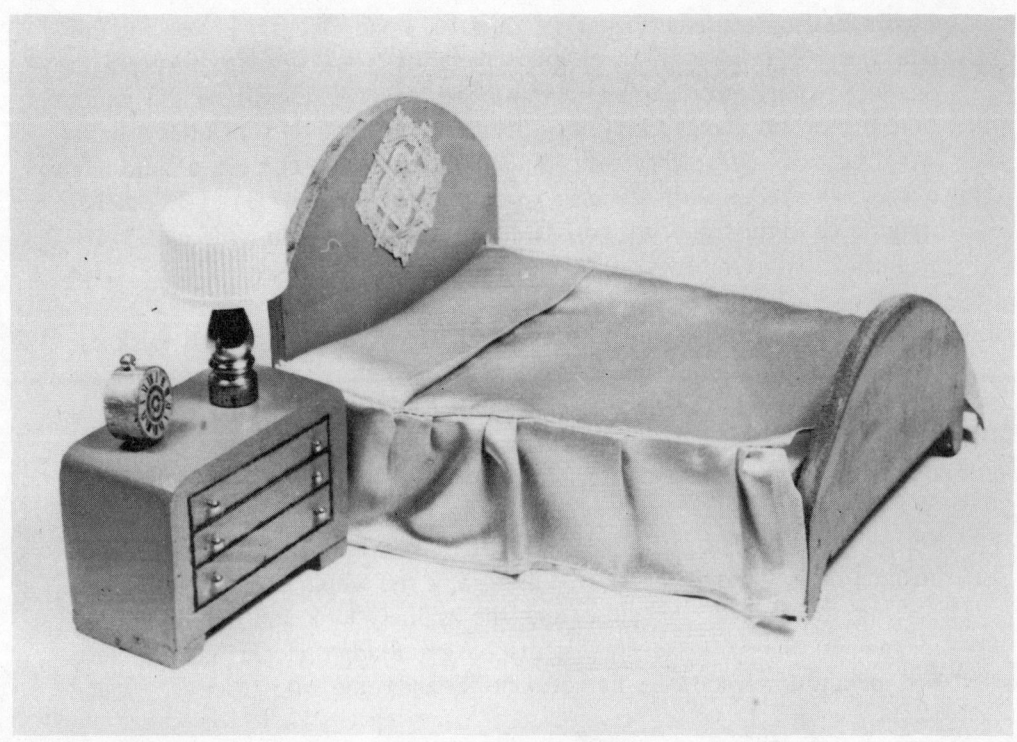

Bed and Nightstand

For the nightstand, use the piece of hardwood you had cut to 2-1/2 inches and 1-1/4 inches. The side that measures 1-1/2 inches will be your height. Round off the two top edges with sandpaper. For legs, cut pieces of balsa wood 1/4 of an inch wide and 1-1/4-inches long. Glue beneath the nightstand. Paint the whole piece brown. Using a ball-point pen and a ruler, make three drawers, 2-inches wide and 3/8 of an inch high. Use brass nails for drawer handles.

DRESSER AND MIRROR

No dollhouse bedroom is complete without a dresser to hold the imaginary clothes and a mirror for primping. This dresser, painted brown to match the bed, was made from the piece of hardwood cut to a size of 2-1/4 inches by 4 inches. Cut legs from balsa wood, making them 1-1/2-inches long by 5/8 of an inch wide. Glue to the bottom of the dresser. Smooth off the two top edges with sandpaper. Paint the dresser brown at this point. For the drawers, use a ball-point pen and a ruler, making the two bottom drawers each 3-3/4-inches wide by 1/2-inch high. The

Dresser and Mirror

three top drawers should be 1-inch wide by 1/2-inch high. Use brass nails for drawer handles.

For the mirror, use a regular pocket mirror and glue this to a piece of heavy cardboard that measures 1/4 of an inch more than your mirror all around. For a frame, use balsa strips that are 1/4 of an inch wide, gluing them to the cardboard and painting them brown. Hang the mirror above the dresser with two-sided mounting tape.

ROCKING CRADLE

Many contemporary nurseries have replaced the cradle with cribs, but dollhouse owners seem reluctant to make the switch. This cradle started with two pieces of 3/16-inch-thick balsa wood cut to 2-1/2-inches wide by 1-1/2-inches high. Using the pattern provided, cut the two end pieces to match. For the bottom of the cradle, use 1/8-inch-thick balsa and cut a piece 1-inch wide by 2-1/2-inches long. Make two shallow cuts into the ends of the cradle, each one 1-inch wide. Put glue on the ends of the

Rocking Cradle

bottom, insert into the cuts, and let dry. For the sides, cut two pieces of the 1/8-inch-thick balsa, each one 2-1/4-inches long by 7/8 of an inch wide. Glue to the bottom and ends of the cradle, forming the sides of the bed. Paint the cradle blue and decorate with hand painted designs.

Summary

Although you have come to the end of this book, it should only be the beginning of many new experiences in creating miniatures. From these ideas, you may go on to develop your own. Creativity is hard to control. There are hundreds of possibilities in these basic instructions.

There are many reasons for making miniatures. The most common reason, of course, is an effort to furnish a special dollhouse for a young relative. These miniatures will increase in value with the years, not only because they are handmade, but also as a remembrance. Who doesn't treasure something made by her mother or favorite aunt? There are also many reasons for making these miniatures for yourself. One woman, who recently furnished an eight-room dollhouse with hundreds of items she had made herself, had started her hobby because her doctor told her to "slow down." Another friend has always been interested in history and finds satisfaction in filling miniature rooms with period pieces, and making appropriate accessories.

These miniatures also make excellent gifts, since they really have no age limit. Several items might be made for a small scene under a plastic dome for an older woman, and it isn't hard to find a young daughter of a friend who has a special interest in her dollhouse and would appreciate handcrafted additions. Giving these miniatures has many added rewards. Not only is the price of the finished product incredibly small, but you also save hours of hunting through stores for just the right gift. In addition, you are giving of your time and energy, which is always appreciated.

Whatever your reason for making these miniatures, you will probably find great interest in this activity. More and more people are becoming concerned with their leisure time. In an effort to conserve energy, people are driving less and interests in hobbies are on the increase. People are looking for entertainment that is inexpensive, relaxing, and yet fulfilling. Making your own miniatures can fill this need. Jean Latham, the British author of *Doll's Houses,* says that in America, ". . . doll's house collecting is on a scale comparable to the eighteenth century craze." May this new craze and this book bring you many pleasurable hours.

Bibliography

Bradford, Faith. *The Dolls' House.* Washington, D. C.: Smithsonian Publication, 1965.
Jacobs, Flora. *A World of Doll Houses.* New York: Gramercy Publishing Co., 1965.
Latham, Jean. *Doll's Houses.* New York: Charles Scribner's Sons, 1969.
Moore, Colleen. *Colleen Moore's Doll House.* New York: Doubleday and Co.